Cameroon

Cameroon

BY PATRICIA K. KUMMER

Enchantment of the World
Second Series

Children's Press®
A Division of Scholastic Inc.

NEW YORK   TORONTO   LONDON   AUCKLAND   SYDNEY
MEXICO CITY   NEW DELHI   HONG KONG
DANBURY, CONNECTICUT

Frontispiece: Cameroonian in Pouss, Cameroon

Consultant: Edouard Bustin, Professor of Political Science, African Studies Center,
Boston University, Boston, MA

Please note: All statistics are as up-to-date as possible at the time of publication.

Book production by Herman Adler Design

Library of Congress Cataloging-in-Publication Data

Kummer, Patricia K.
Cameroon / by Patricia K. Kummer.
    p. cm. — (Enchantment of the world. Second series)
Includes bibliographical references and index.
    ISBN 0-516-24256-3
1. Cameroon—Juvenile literature. [1. Cameroon.] I. Title. II. Series.
DT564.K86 2004
967.11—dc22   2003019634

Acknowledgments

I would like to thank the staffs of the Melville J. Herskovits Library of African Studies at Northwestern University in Evanston, Illinois, and the Ryerson and Burnham Libraries of the Art Institute of Chicago for their gracious assistance. In addition, my thanks are extended to the staff at the Lisle Library District, my home library, for quickly putting through my numerous interlibrary loan requests and for going the extra mile to obtain the sources that were hard to find.

Cover photo:
Bamiléké masked dancers

Contents

Tribal huts

Fulani men

Africa in Miniature

MASKED DANCERS, SOME ON STILTS, WHIRL ABOUT AT village festivals. Wooden flutes and xylophones made from gourds fill the air with music. A small audience gathers around a storyteller who recites an ancient tale. Men in long white robes enter a mosque to pray. Families in Western dress attend Catholic or Protestant services. Men or women with special skills perform traditional healing rituals. People from all of Cameroon's ethnic groups take part in these activities. The sounds of their many African languages, plus French and English, are heard as Cameroonians go about their daily life. Pygmies still hunt and grow crops in the southern rain forest. Fulani herd cattle in the north. Many Cameroonians work in the oil and shipping industries. These are just a few examples of the variety of life in Cameroon. Indeed, Cameroon is "Africa in Miniature."

Cameroon's tourism slogan, "Africa in Miniature," accurately describes this West African country. While traveling through Cameroon, visitors experience much of Africa's geographic, cultural, and historical

Opposite: **A traditional festival in western Cameroon**

Boys from the Mbuti pygmy tribe hunt in the rain forest.

Cameroon's landscape varies from coastal lowlands to deserts to mountain highlands.

variety. Geographically, Cameroon has coastal lowlands, mountain highlands, plateaus, and plains. Beaches, grasslands, rain forest, savanna, and desert cover the land. The variety of landforms and altitudes creates several climate zones with many different kinds of plants and animals.

Causes of Cultural and Historical Diversity

For thousands of years, African people crossed through what is today called Cameroon. They traveled from the east, west, and north. Many of them settled in this part of Africa. Today, people from more than two hundred different ethnic groups live in Cameroon. Each group speaks its own distinct language. Many ethnic groups also follow traditional religious beliefs and hand down the arts, crafts, and music of their ancestors. Some ethnic groups in northern Cameroon are Muslim and follow the religious teachings of Islam.

Besides Cameroon's many African peoples, European explorers, traders, and colonizers also left their marks. Cameroon shares much of the same colonial experience of other former African colonies. However, Cameroon was ruled by not one but three European powers—first by Germany, followed by France and Great Britain. For more than forty years, Cameroon was divided into two uneven parts. The western one-fifth was British Cameroons, and the eastern four-fifths became French Cameroun. Today, Cameroon is the only African country to have both French and English as official languages. The Europeans also brought their forms of Christianity to Cameroon. Many Cameroonians in the southern part of the country are Roman Catholic or belong to a Protestant church.

The Fulani make up more than 9 percent of Cameroon's population. This is a Fulani holy man.

Establishing a Cameroonian Identity

The variety and diversity found in Cameroon provide an exciting and colorful experience for visitors. However, the same variety and diversity have caused problems for Cameroon. It has been difficult to achieve a national Cameroonian identity because Cameroonians share so little in common. After more than forty years of independence, divisions among Cameroonians remain to this day. Language and colonial history divide the country between the English-speaking western provinces and the French-speaking east. Religion also splits Cameroon between the Muslim north and the predominantly Christian south. Then, of course, there are the differences among Cameroon's many ethnic groups.

Even the country's official name and form of government have changed more than once since achieving independence. People in other nations, as well as Cameroonians themselves, thus have a hard time understanding what Cameroon is.

In spite of these problems, Cameroon's government has taken steps to establish a national identity for the people and country. First, Cameroon became a unitary republic with a strong central government that formulates laws for the entire country. So Cameroon differs from the United States, which has a strong federal government but also has fifty states, each with its own state government. Second, the government has maintained peace, for the most part, among Cameroon's many ethnic groups. Third, the strong, stable government and social peace have paved the way for relative prosperity for most Cameroonians.

By rallying around the goals of peace, stability, and prosperity, Cameroonians are beginning to form a national identity. They know that to achieve and to maintain these goals they must work together as Cameroonians. The Indomitable Lions, Cameroon's national soccer team, provides another source of national identity. Most Cameroonians support this winning team. While establishing national unity

A Cameroonian holds high the country's flag, displaying pride in her country.

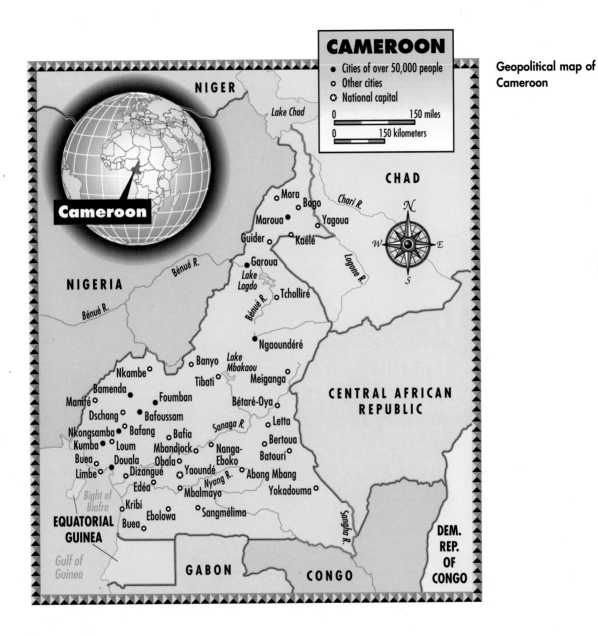

CAMEROON

- Cities of over 50,000 people
- Other cities
- National capital

0   150 miles
0   150 kilometers

NIGER

Lake Chad

CHAD

Mora

Bago

Chari R.

Maroua

Yagoua

Guider

Kaélé

Garoua

Lake
Lagdo

NIGERIA

Bénué R.

Logone R.

Tcholliré

Bénué R.

Bénué R.

Ngaoundéré

Banyo

Lake
Mbakaou

Nkambe

Tibati

Meiganga

CENTRAL AFRICAN
REPUBLIC

Bamenda

Foumban

Mamfé

Bétaré-Oya

Dschang

Bafoussam

Sanaga R.

Letta

Nkongsamba

Bafang

Bafia

Kumba

Loum

Mbandjock

Nanga-
Eboko

Bertoua

Batouri

Buea

Douala

Obala

Abong Mbang

Limbe

Dizangué

Yaoundé

Nyong R.

Bight of
Biafra

Edéa

Mbalmayo

Yokadouma

Kribi

Ebolowa

Sangmélima

EQUATORIAL
GUINEA

Buea

Sangha R.

DEM.
REP.
OF
CONGO

Gulf of
Guinea

GABON

CONGO

and a national identity, however, Cameroonians are trying not
to lose the richness of their heritage. Most hope that they will
achieve a workable balance. In that way, Cameroon will still
be Africa in Miniature.

The Hinge
of Africa

Fishermen's boats line the coast of the Bight of Biafra.

CAMEROON'S LOCATION HAS GIVEN THE COUNTRY ANOTHER nickname—the Hinge of Africa—because it links West Africa and Central Africa. Although Cameroon is usually identified as a Central African country, sometimes it is grouped with the countries of West Africa. The West African country of Nigeria lies to the west of Cameroon. The Central African countries of Chad, Central African Republic, and Congo Republic are Cameroon's eastern neighbors. Congo also borders Cameroon to the south, as do the Central Africa countries of Gabon and Equatorial Guinea.

Bodies of water also form Cameroon's borders. To the southwest is the Bight of Biafra, which is a large bay in the Gulf of Guinea. At the northern tip of Cameroon lies Lake Chad, which Cameroon shares with Chad, Niger, and Nigeria. Rivers mark Cameroon's borders at several places to the east, south, and west.

Opposite: **The Mandara Mountains are a volcanic range that run 120 miles (193 km) along the Nigeria-Cameroon border.**

Cameroon's Geographic Features

Area: 183,569 square miles (475,442 sq km)

Greatest Distance East to West: 446 miles (718 km)

Greatest Distance North to South: 749 miles (1,205 km)

Longest Shared Border: 1,050 miles (1,690 km), with Nigeria

Highest Elevation: Mount Cameroon at 13,435 feet (4,095 m) above sea level, the highest point in West Africa

Lowest Elevation: Sea level at the coastline of the Bight of Biafra

Longest River: Sanaga River at 569 miles (916 km)

Coastline: 250 miles (402 km)

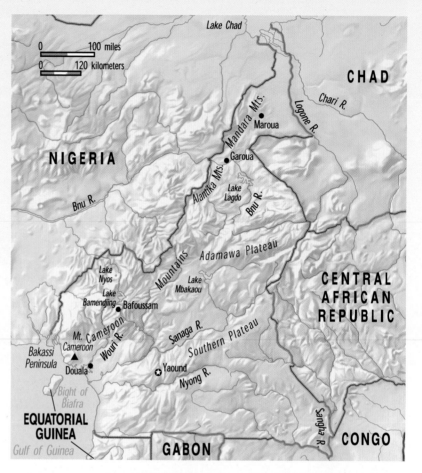

Average Annual Temperatures: 82°F (27.8°C) in January in the northern savanna; 70°F (21.1°C) in July on the central plateau

Highest Annual Precipitation: 405 inches (1,029 cm), at Debundscha Point on Mount Cameroon; one of the world's wettest spots

Triangular in shape, Cameroon is a bit larger than the state of California, the third largest state in the United States. Compared with other African countries, however, Cameroon's 183,569 square miles (475,442 square kilometers) make it a medium-sized country. Many different kinds of landforms, climates, soils, vegetation, and bodies of water, nevertheless, are packed into the four topographic areas of Cameroon. They range from coastal lowlands to West Africa's highest mountains. Most of Cameroon, however, is made up of plateaus and plains.

Cameroon coast at Kribi

The Coastal Lowlands

Between Cameroon's border with Equatorial Guinea and Nigeria lie the coastal lowlands. This land rises from sea level along the coast to about 1,000 feet (305 meters) above sea level inland. The coastal lowlands stretch inland on average only about 250 miles (402 km). Near the city of Douala the lowlands widen to about 50 miles (80 km), but close to Equatorial Guinea they narrow to about 5 miles (8 km) wide. White sand beaches near the city of Kribi touch the Bight of Biafra. Farther north, black sand beaches line the coast near the city of Limbe. The black sand is a result of seawater breaking down lava from volcanic eruptions of nearby Mount Cameroon.

Mangrove swamps cover about 30 percent of Cameroon's coastal area.

Swampland covers much of the rest of the coastal lowlands. Small streams and wide rivers cut through the swamps as they make their way to the Bight of Biafra. Large stands of mangrove trees grow in the swamps. Trees that produce food crops of palm oil, cocoa, bananas, and tea also grow on the coastal plain. Rubber trees produce materials used in industry. Oil and natural gas are the main mineral resources of the coastal lowlands.

Western Mountain Ranges

Cameroon's mountains extend southwest to northeast close to the western border with Nigeria. From the south, these mountains are the Cameroon, Alantika, and Mandara ranges. All of these mountains contain volcanoes. The Cameroon Mountains are the country's highest range. Within them is Mount Cameroon. This is the highest point in West Africa, even though it actually stands in the coastal lowland. Mount Cameroon is also Cameroon's only active volcano. The last time it erupted was in 2000.

The Cameroon Mountains are home to many endangered species such as chimpanzees and gorillas.

The volcanic soil in western Cameroon yields large crops. This is especially true in the area called the Bamenda Grasslands. These grasslands lie between the northern Cameroon Mountains and Nigeria. Arabica coffee trees, beans, cassava, groundnuts (a plant with edible tubers, such as peanuts), maize (corn), sugarcane, and yams grow well there. The Bamenda Grasslands also have several good-sized towns and cities, including Bafoussam, Bamenda, and Foumban. Other volcanic grasslands lie at the base of the Mandara Mountains. The city of Garoua is the southern gateway to these mountains.

The volcanic soil of the Bamenda Grasslands is very fertile and well suited for growing crops.

Lake Nyos is inside a volcanic crater that was formed about four hundred years ago. It is about 5,900 feet (1,800 m) wide and 682 feet (208 m) deep.

Several of Cameroon's rivers have their source in the western mountains. The Wouri River flows southeast through Douala into the Bight of Biafra. The Cross River flows west, and the Metchum River flows northwest. Both of them enter Nigeria. Many lakes formed in the craters of volcanoes are also in this area of Cameroon. They include Lake Nyos, Lake Barombi Mbo, and Awing Lake. The Manengouba Crater lakes, Man Lake and Woman Lake, are both considered sacred. Woman Lake is the larger of the two, and the water looks blue. The water in Man Lake looks green.

Cameroon's Worst Natural Disaster

On August 21, 1986, carbon dioxide gas exploded from Lake Nyos, a volcanic crater lake in Northwest Province. The cloud of gas rolled down into nearby villages and suffocated about 1,700 people as they slept. Because oxygen was squeezed from the air by the heavier carbon dioxide, the villagers could not breathe. Besides the people, many animals, from ants to cattle, also died. In 1984, a similar explosion had occurred at Lake Monoun. There, the gas killed about forty people.

Scientists have not yet figured out what caused these explosions. They do know that springs heavily charged with carbon dioxide feed into the lakes. In 2001, a team of Cameroonian, French, Japanese, and U.S. scientists and engineers began degassing the lakes. Pipes were sunk into the water to pump out carbon dioxide and gradually release it into the air. Mixed with water, the gas shoots upward like a geyser through the pipes (right). A landslide or movement underground, however, could trigger another explosion.

The Plateau Region

In the middle of Cameroon stand two groups of plateaus—the Southern Plateau and the Adamawa Plateau. The Southern Plateau is north of the coastal lowlands and east of the Cameroon Mountains. This plateau's average elevation is about 3,000 feet (914 m) above sea level. Major rivers of the Southern Plateau include the Sanaga, Nyong, and Campo. These rivers tumble from the plateau over steep falls before they reach the coastal lowlands. From there, they all flow into the Bight of Biafra. Dams and hydroelectric power stations have been built at the Edea, Song Loulou, and Nachtigal Falls on the Sanaga River.

Cameroon's rain forest covers the Southern Plateau. Food crops that flourish in the rain forest include cocoa, oil palms, coffee, groundnuts, and yams. In the midst of the rain forest, Yaoundé, Cameroon's capital city, has grown and developed. Smaller rain forest cities include Bertoua and Ebolowa.

North of the Southern Plateau, the Adamawa Plateau rises. This plateau stretches from east to west across Cameroon and extends into Nigeria. The average elevation of this plateau is about 4,500 feet (1,372 m) above sea level. On the Adamawa Plateau, Cameroon's humid, forested areas in the south give way to drier, temperate savanna land in the north. This plateau is also Cameroon's main watershed. Major rivers with their sources on the plateau flow in all directions. The Sanaga flows southeast; the Bénué, northwest into Nigeria. The Mbéré flows northeast, forming part of Cameroon's border with the Central African Republic before entering Chad.

Oil palms usually grow among the other trees of the rain forest. Here, though, is an oil palm plantation.

Wheat, other grains, and groundnuts are the main crops on the Adamawa Plateau. Cattle, sheep, and goats graze on its savanna grasses. Bauxite and tin are this plateau's main mineral deposits. Ngaoundéré is the largest city on the plateau.

Sheep graze on the Adamawa Plateau.

The Northern Plains

Between the Adamawa Plateau and Lake Chad lie the Northern Plains. This area is also called the Chad Basin. In a basin, waters have no way to reach the sea. In the Chad Basin, all water drains into Lake Chad. Most of this lake actually lies in Nigeria and Chad, with the lake's northern tip in Niger. Cameroon's northern rivers—the Chari and the Logone—are the main sources of Lake Chad's water, however. In the 1960s, Lake Chad was Africa's fourth largest lake. Now it is Africa's sixth largest because it has shrunk by more than 90 percent. Drought, evaporation, and irrigation are believed to be responsible for Lake Chad's decrease in size.

Cameroon's River Systems

Cameroon's river systems are another reason for the country's nickname of Hinge of Africa. Cameroon is the dividing line for the Niger River Basin and the Congo River Basin. The water from rivers that flow west out of Cameroon, eventually emptying into the Niger River in Nigeria, make Cameroon part of the Niger River Basin. Cameroon's Niger Basin rivers include the Bénué in the north and the Katsina in the southwest. Water from rivers that run southeast from Cameroon finds its way into the Congo River in Congo. Some southeastern-flowing rivers in Cameroon are the Kadei, Dja, Boumba, and Ngoko.

The arid landscape of Cameroon's Northern Plains

Some parts of the Northern Plains have low, rolling hills. Other areas are flat. The soil in this part of Cameroon is for the most part poor for growing crops. However, the soil does produce good crops of cotton and groundnuts. Lands to the east along the Chari and Logone rivers become flooded during the rainy season. From these rivers and from Lake Chad, catches of fish provide a good source of protein food for the local population. Maroua, Kousseri, and Waza are major cities of the Northern Plains.

Three Climates

Cameroon is between about 2 degrees and 12 degrees north of the equator. This location gives the country an equatorial or tropical climate with year-round high temperatures. However, the country's varying rainfall has formed three different tropical climate zones: the southern tropical rain forest, the central tropical savanna, and the northern semiarid plains. Cameroon's seasons are based on when the rain falls. Rather than seasons of spring, summer, winter, and fall, Cameroon has rainy and dry seasons.

The coastal lowlands and the Southern Plateau's rain forest are in the southern tropical rain forest zone. This part of Cameroon is hot and humid all year. The average daily high June temperature in Douala and Yaoundé is about 82° Fahrenheit (28° Celsius). There really isn't a dry season, just a few months with less rain. From north to south, this zone receives from 60 inches (152 centimeters) to 160 inches (406 cm) of rain each year. The humidity is about 80 percent year-round. However, Yaoundé and other places at higher elevations are more comfortable, with less humidity.

Cameroon's tropical savanna climate is found on the Adamawa Plateau. This drier zone has a rainy season that lasts from April through October. About 60 inches (152 cm) of rain fall in this zone each year. The dry season lasts from November through March. Temperatures can reach 95°F (35°C) in March.

In the semiarid north, rain falls from May through September. This rainfall ranges from about 40 inches (102 cm) near Garoua to about 30 inches (76 cm) near Kousseri. During the dry season from October through April, temperatures can soar above 100°F (38°C) for long stretches. High temperatures and little rain turn the area's riverbeds to cracked earth. When it does rain, the rivers overflow their banks.

During the dry season, hot, dry harmattan winds blow down from the Sahara. These winds cover everything—plants, animals, buildings, and people—with a reddish-brown dust. The harmattan affects northern Cameroon the most but also reaches far south. Less rain falls there during the harmattan.

A road has flooded and become impassable due to heavy rains.

Looking at Cameroon's Cities

Douala, the capital of the Littoral Province, is Cameroon's largest city (below). Located at the mouth of the Wouri River on Cameroon's coast, Douala is also the country's largest seaport. European traders had their first contact with what is now Cameroon through the area's Duala chiefs. Named for the Duala ethnic group, the city today is known as Cameroon's economic and industrial capital. Residents can shop in large department stores and supermarkets, as well as in outdoor markets. The markets offer everything from fresh fruits and vegetables to Cameroonian textiles, masks, art, and jewelry. Consulates of foreign countries and offices of many multinational companies are also in Douala. In addition to the original Duala population, large numbers of Bamiléké people live in Douala. The city's climate is hot and humid, with annual rainfall of 160 inches (406 cm) and average high daily temperatures of 85°F (29°C).

North of Douala is Bafoussam, Cameroon's fifth largest city (above). Bafoussam is the capital of West Province and is the center of the Bamiléké ethnic group. Visitors can tour the *chefferie*, or chief's compound. This is a good example of Bamiléké architecture. Bafoussam is in one of Cameroon's major cocoa and arabica coffee-producing areas. Main industries in Bafoussam include a coffee-processing plant, a brewery, and a printing press. Good paved roads lead into and out of the city in many directions.

Northwest of Bafoussam is Garoua, Cameroon's third largest city and the capital of North Province. Located on the Bénué River, Garoua is Cameroon's third largest port. Cotton from nearby fields is processed in the city. A brewery and soap plant are other industries in Garoua. The Fulani are the city's main ethnic group. Other Muslim residents include the Hausa and Bornu. They pray in Cameroon's largest mosque, the Grande Mosquée in Garoua. Cameroon's first president, Ahmadou Ahidjo, came from this city. Under his rule, starting in 1960, Garoua experienced great growth and development.

Farther north is Maroua, Cameroon's fourth largest city and the capital of Extreme North Province. The Mayo Kaliao River, which is dry for about half the year, runs through the city. Mainly a Fulani/Muslim city, Maroua attracts non-Muslim groups on Mondays—the main market day. Near the market is the Musée du Diamaré that displays Sao and Fulani civilization artifacts. In the museum, there is a craft market where locally made leather bags, sandals, and floor cushions are sold. Other local industries produce cotton cloth and cotton oil. Maroua's crafters are also known for their pottery, jewelry, and metalwork.

A Changing Natural Environment

CAMEROON'S VARIOUS LANDFORMS AND CLIMATE ZONES have created a rich natural environment. Different kinds of plants grow in each climate zone. The plants, in turn, provide food and homes to a variety of animals. Since the early years of colonization, however, Cameroon's natural environment has undergone many changes. In the southwest, trees were cut down to make way for plantations. Throughout the country, animals were hunted for their skins. Their heads were mounted as trophies. During the late 1900s, the logging industry cut down huge areas of trees in the southeastern rain forest. Gorillas, monkeys, and many types of birds were driven from their homes.

In recent years, Cameroon's government, the Worldwide Fund for Nature (WWF), and other international groups have taken steps to protect Cameroon's natural environment. The government has set aside reserves of protected forestland. It

Opposite: **This giraffe is protected in Cameroon's Waza National Park.**

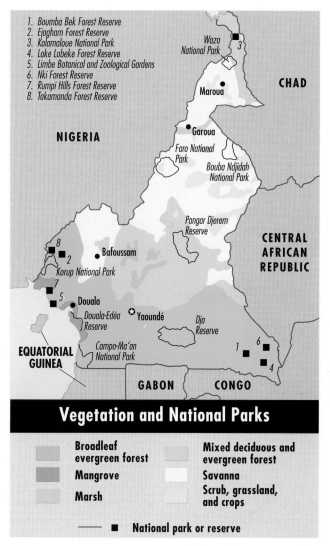

1. Boumba Bek Forest Reserve
2. Ejagham Forest Reserve
3. Kalamaloue National Park
4. Lake Lobeke Forest Reserve
5. Limbe Botanical and Zoological Gardens
6. Nki Forest Reserve
7. Rumpi Hills Forest Reserve
8. Takamanda Forest Reserve

Vegetation and National Parks

- Broadleaf evergreen forest
- Mangrove
- Marsh
- Mixed deciduous and evergreen forest
- Savanna
- Scrub, grassland, and crops
- ■ National park or reserve

also began a five-year plan of replanting to replace felled trees. In addition, Cameroon's government established several national parks as wildlife reserves. Teams of WWF researchers set up camps in the forest reserves to monitor environmental conditions for plants and animals.

Forestlands: Trees, Animals, Parks, and Reserves

Two kinds of forests cover Cameroon's coastal lowlands and much of the Southern Plateau. Mangrove forests are found in the swampy lands along the coast. Rhizophora and avicennia are the main types of mangrove trees. These trees have long roots that extend from their trunks into swampy water. The roots are visible above the water and look like legs. These trees look almost as if they were walking. Raffia palms and oil palms also grow in the swamps. Birds seen in the swamps include flamingos, ibis, kingfishers, and storks. As is true of

Kingfishers (left) and storks (right) are common throughout Cameroon's swamps.

most swamps, mosquitoes are a problem in this part of Cameroon. Bites from anopheles mosquitoes can transmit malaria. Rivers on the coastal lowlands contain shrimp and prawns. Fish as small as sardines and as huge as sharks swim farther out in coastal waters.

Across southern Cameroon in the east and inland from the coast in the west, rain forest covers the land. This is the northwestern part of the Congo Basin rain forest that spans five other countries. Since 1980 about 4.8 million acres (1.9 million hectares) of Cameroon's rain forest have been cut down. That leaves about 40.8 million acres (16.5 million ha). At one time, however, Cameroon's rain forest covered about 86.4 million acres (35 million ha). Hardwood trees such as ebony, iroko, obeche, and mahogany grow in Cameroon's rain forest. Because wood products from these trees are very valuable, logging is a big business in Cameroon.

Though Cameroon's rain forests spread over 40 million acres (about 16 million ha), they once covered about 86 million acres (35 million ha).

A herd of elephants drinks and bathes at a watering hole in Waza National Park.

Southeastern Cameroon has the country's last areas of untouched rain forest. The Dja Reserve is the largest of these. Farther east are the Nki and Boumba Bek Forest Reserves. Lake Lobeke Forest Reserve borders reserves in Central African Republic and Congo. This is Africa's largest area of protected rain forest. Primates, including chimpanzees, gorillas, mandrills, and monkeys, share these reserves with forest elephants and buffalo. Hornbills, parrots, and toucans are just a few of the birds in the reserves.

West of the Dja Forest Reserve is Campo-Ma'an National Park. It was established to protect the rain forest that is close to Cameroon's far southeastern coast. The thick vegetation hides the park's animals, such as buffalo, elephants, and mandrills.

Bush Meat Hunting

Bush meat is the meat from any wild animal. Restaurants in Cameroon's cities like to have it on their menus. Bush meat, especially that of gorillas, chimpanzees, and elephants, is considered a delicacy. Hunting in Cameroon requires a permit, and it is not allowed within protected lands. Most bush meat hunting, however, is illegal. In and near Korup National Park, some families earn about one-third of their income from bush meat hunting. In the Dja Reserve, money from the sale of bush meat is second only to income from farming cocoa. With chimpanzee bringing as much as U.S.$25 for a piece of meat, it's not surprising that bush meat hunting is so popular. However, the practice is endangering some of Cameroon's special animals.

Takamanda and Ejagham Forest Reserves and Korup National Park line much of Cameroon's southwestern border with Nigeria. Lowland gorillas live in the Takamanda Forest.

Lowland gorillas can be found in Cameroon's forest reserves.

Korup National Park was established in 1986. The rain forest within the park is believed to be the oldest in Africa. About four hundred different kinds of trees are part of it. More than one-fourth of Africa's primate species live among these trees. They include chimpanzees, lowland gorillas, and monkeys. Several kinds of pesky insects are found in the park, too. Sweat bees and driver ants can sting and bite. Blackflies leave itchy bites on swimmers in the park's rivers. Korup Park also

The duiker antelope can be found roaming Cameroon feeding on leaves, seeds, flowers, and fruits.

supports more than three hundred different kinds of birds, including blue cuckoo-shrikes, long-tailed hawks, and rufous-sided broadbills. The Rumpi Hills Forest Reserve is south of Korup. Duiker antelope live at ground level while red colobus monkeys make homes in the treetops. To the southeast is Lake Barombi Mbo. Dikume, kululu, pungu, and pindu are fish found only in this lake. These small fish breed by keeping fertilized eggs in their mouth until they hatch. Catfish also live in Lake Barombi Mbo.

The red colubus monkey spends its days high among the treetops.

The Tsetse Fly

Cameroon has some of the world's largest animals—elephants, giraffes, lions. Although they are big and some harmful to people, they usually do not pose a threat. A bite from the tiny tsetse fly, however, can lead to sleeping sickness. The tsetse fly lives mainly near rivers and streams in heavily forested areas in eastern Cameroon. People who live or work in the forests, as well as visitors to forest reserves, should quickly take proper medicine when they are bitten. If untreated, sleeping sickness can lead to inflammation of the brain and then death.

Limbe Botanical and Zoological Gardens

The Limbe Botanical and Zoological Gardens (LBZG) traces its history back to 1892. Paul Preuss, a German horticulturist, established the gardens to grow and to study agricultural crops and trees. In 1963, the Limbe Zoo was founded. Today, the zoo is called the Limbe Wildlife Center (LWC). The change in name marks a change in its purpose. Limbe is no longer a place where people are just entertained by watching animals. Instead, the LWC focuses on educating people, preserving animals in the wild, and conserving their environment.

The Preuss monkey and the red-eared monkey are endangered species cared for at LWC. Other primates at LWC are drill monkeys, western lowland gorillas, and chimpanzees. The world's largest and smallest crocodiles also live at LWC. The Nile crocodile (left) is the largest; the dwarf crocodile, the smallest. The Gabon viper, a poisonous snake with the world's largest fangs, also is at the LWC.

Another part of the LBZG is the herbarium with more than 2,300 different kinds of butterflies. The chamehoe beckari and papilio zororates are butterflies found only in Cameroon. The LBZG also has a huge plant collection that includes mangrove and hardwood trees, ferns, orchids, fruits, and such spices as cinnamon and nutmeg—all from Cameroon.

Savannas: Grasses, Wildlife, and National Parks

The rest of Cameroon, north of the rain forest, is savanna. *Savanna* is another word for grassland. Cameroon has three kinds of savannas. The savanna directly north of the rain forests still has many trees. However, there are more grasses under them than in the rain forest. Farther north, the land is covered with tall grasses and some trees. This is similar to parts of the prairies and plains in the Midwest of the United States. Raffia palm bushes are common in this part of the savanna. In the far north, the savanna becomes little more than small clumps of short grass because of high temperatures and little rain. However, tall grasses grow in the swampy land along Lake Chad and the Logone River.

Some of Cameroon's most varied wildlife live on the savanna. Antelopes, elephants, giraffes, hippopotamuses, lions, rhinoceroses, and various birds can be sighted there. Most of them now live in national parks in Cameroon's northern savanna. Wildlife is not always protected, however, in Cameroon's parks. Poachers have killed most of the animals at Faro National Park. Many kinds of antelope, such as hartebeests, kobs, and waterbucks, live in Bénué National Park. Hippopotamuses and crocodiles swim in the Bénué River.

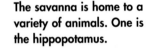

The savanna is home to a variety of animals. One is the hippopotamus.

Along the river's banks, birds such as bat hawks, Egyptian plovers, and grey pratincoles can be seen. Bouba Ndjidah National Park is nearby to the east. This park was formed in 1968 to protect black rhinoceroses. There are very few of these animals left, and Bouba Ndjidah is the only place where they live in Cameroon. The thick grasses in the park hide leopards and lions. Buffaloes and elephants are more easily seen. Farther north is Waza National Park. Most of Cameroon's giraffes gracefully lope across the short grasses in this park. Elephants and lions also live in Waza. Arabian bustards, ostriches, and scissor-tailed kites are a few of the birds found in Waza. Still farther north is Cameroon's smallest and newest national park—Kalamaloue National Park. Here crocodiles and hippopotamuses swim in the Chari River.

A highly threatened animal is the black rhino. Cameroon has taken measures to protect the black rhino by placing them in Bouba Ndjidah National Park.

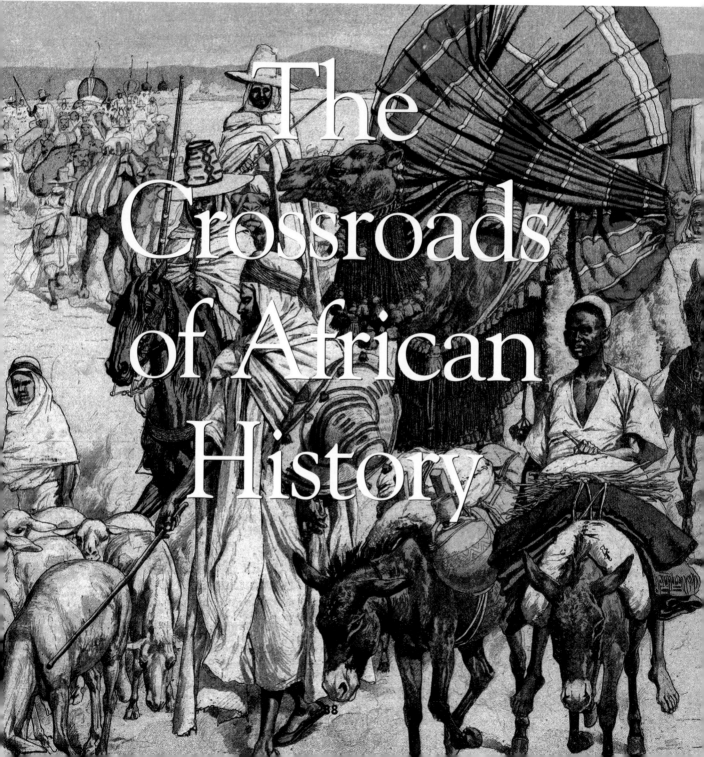

The Crossroads of African History

ARCHAEOLOGISTS AND HISTORIANS BELIEVE THAT PEOPLE have lived in what is now Cameroon for at least 50,000 years. The Baka Pygmies in Cameroon's southeastern rain forests are descendants of those early people. During those many thousands of years, other groups moved south and east into and across Cameroon. Bantu-speaking people from present-day Nigeria moved east into Cameroon about 3,000 years ago, driving the Pygmy people south. The Bantu brought iron-making skills with them and used iron tools to cut paths through the rain forest. Today, most ethnic groups in Cameroon speak Bantu languages. They include people in the Duala and the Fang ethnic groups.

This drawing illustrates Hanno's exploration of Africa's west coast.

The earliest recorded history of Cameroon is in the writings of Hanno, a Carthaginian explorer and sailor. He led an expedition from present-day Tunisia down the coast of West Africa. Arriving off the coast of Cameroon about 500 B.C., he and his crew saw an eruption of Mount Cameroon. Hanno called the mountain "The Chariot of the Gods."

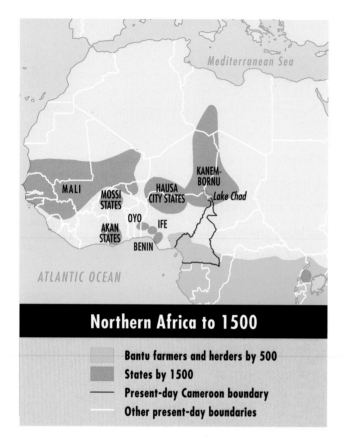

Northern Africa to 1500

▫ Bantu farmers and herders by 500

▪ States by 1500

— Present-day Cameroon boundary

— Other present-day boundaries

The trans-Sahara slave trade brought Africans north to the Islamic world.

In northern Cameroon during the 400s B.C., the Sao people built a thriving civilization near Lake Chad and present-day Kousseri. They had moved southwest from the Nile River valley. The Sao, ruled by a king, were skilled producers of pottery and of bronze and copper goods.

By the A.D. 800s, Arab traders crossed the Sahara and exchanged goods with the Sao. One kind of "goods" that the Arabs later took north with them was human captives, or slaves. Slaves taken from Cameroon were part of the flourishing trans-Sahara slave trade. Historians estimate that about 10,000 slaves a year crossed north over the desert—many of them from Cameroon. People sold into slavery at that time were not slaves for life. They could work and buy their freedom, or gain freedom by marrying a free person.

The Arabs also brought their Islamic religion to northern Cameroon. Many Sao people, as well as others with whom the Arabs came into contact, in time converted to Islam. By the 1400s, the Sao civilization gave way to the Kanem-Bornu Empire. Between the 1400s and 1600s, the Fulani began moving east from present-day Senegal toward Cameroon. The Arabs had brought Islam to these West African people also.

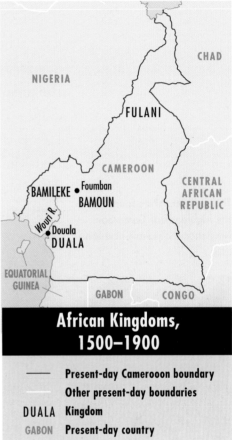

African Kingdoms, 1500–1900

	Present-day Camerooon boundary
	Other present-day boundaries
DUALA	Kingdom
GABON	Present-day country

Cameroon's Kingdoms

By the 1700s, the Fulani had settled in northern Cameroon. Known mainly as cattle herders, many Fulani also lived in towns. In the early 1800s, the Fulani gained control of Cameroon north of the Adamawa Plateau. In 1806, Modibo Adama (1786–1847), for whom the plateau is named, led a *jihad*, an Islamic holy war. During the jihad the Fulani also pushed into the western grasslands but did not gain control of the area. As a result of the jihad, Adama established the Adamawa Kingdom across northern Cameroon and into Nigeria. The kingdom was a theocracy ruled by Fulanis, who were Islamic holy men.

Throughout northern Cameroon, the Fulani set up *lamidats*. These were political and religious units headed by a *lamido*. The lamido controlled the government and business of the area and led the prayers at the mosque. Within the lamidats, society was divided into free people and slaves. The Fulani, Arabs, and all other Muslims were free people. The non-Muslims whom the Fulani had defeated became slaves. They made up the servant class and could be sold, usually to Arabs in the trans-Sahara trade. Other non-Muslim ethnic groups who lived at the edge of Fulani territory were called Kirdi, or pagans. Today, at least twenty-one lamidats still exist in Cameroon, including the cities of Garoua, Maroua, and Ngaoundéré.

Other kinds of kingdoms developed in southern Cameroon. During the 1500s the Bamiléké formed more than one hundred independent kingdoms in the western grasslands. The kingdoms ranged from fifty to thirty thousand people. Bamiléké rulers or chiefs were called *fons*. The fons were aided by a council of nine nobles, other royals, and members of secret societies. The fon owned all the land in the kingdom and had the power of life and death over the people. Before his death, a fon would appoint one of his sons as his successor.

This ancient shrine found in the highlands of Cameroon was once the palace of a fon.

The lands in Bamiléké kingdoms grew or shrank as a result of war. The kingdoms fought among themselves, as well as against the Fulani and Bamoun. Although the Bamiléké kingdoms successfully fought off Fulani attacks, Bamiléké people were sometimes taken by the Fulani or sold to them as slaves.

The Bamoun kingdom was to the east of the Bamilékés. It was founded by Nshare Yen in the 1400s, with Foumban as the capital. Succeeding kings strengthened the walls around the capital and kept the Fulani out. Bamoun kings expanded their kingdom by pushing into Bamiléké lands. Ibrahim Njoya is thought of as the Bamoun's greatest king (1890–1923). He designed the royal palace that still stands in Foumban, invented the Bamoun alphabet, constructed a mill to grind corn, and established a museum. When Ibrahim Njoya converted to Islam in 1916, his title changed from king to sultan.

The Bamoun kingdom grew and prospered under the rule of Ibrahim Njoya.

Bamoun royal palace

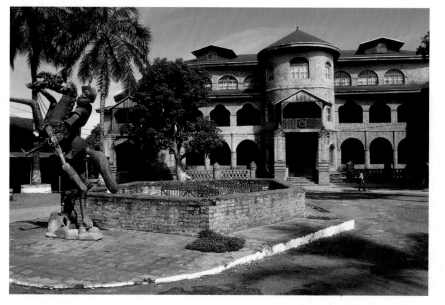

Although there is no longer a Bamoun kingdom, there is a Bamoun sultan, Mboumbou Njoya Ibrahim. He can trace his lineage back to Nshare Yen.

Kingdoms also developed along Cameroon's coast. The most powerful were those of the Duala people. By 1600, the Duala had moved down the Wouri River and settled at its mouth, near present-day Douala. The Duala had two kingdoms—Bell and Akwa—each ruled by a chief. At first, the Duala made their living by fishing and were known for making long dugout canoes. They paddled up the river in them and traded fish for farm crops with inland ethnic groups. By the mid-1600s, they had become middlemen in trade between these ethnic groups and newly arrived Europeans.

European Contact

Cameroon's coast had been untouched by outsiders since Hanno's sighting of Mount Cameroon in 500 B.C. Almost two thousand years later, in 1472, Portuguese explorers landed at the mouth of the Wouri River. The river was full of crayfish, which the Portuguese called prawns (to Western people, a prawn is a type of shrimp). They named the river Rio dos Camarões, or River of Prawns. Soon, the name Camarões came to mean the entire coast of present-day Cameroon.

Portuguese explorers sailed to Africa on caravels.

The Portuguese began successful trading relationships with ethnic groups along the coast. The mangrove swamps, insects, and local diseases, however, kept the Portuguese offshore. Instead, the sailors carried out trade from their ships. The main goods exchanged were African ivory and slaves for European cloth and metal wares.

By the 1600s, the Portuguese had lost control of trade along the Cameroon coast. They were replaced by the Dutch. By the mid-1600s, the Duala emerged as the official middlemen in trade between the Dutch and inland ethnic groups The Dutch also traded from their ships. The Duala carried goods in their dugout canoes to and from the Dutch ships. They exchanged ivory and rubber from inland ethnic groups for European cloth, metal wares, and guns. By the mid-1600s, the main trading goods were slaves. French and English plantation owners in America used slaves to plant and harvest crops. The Duala

This illustration depicts the purchase of slaves on Africa's West Coast.

obtained the slaves from inland chiefs, with the Bamiléké making up large numbers of those slaves.

In the 1700s, British traders replaced the Dutch. The British anglicized the name *Camarões* to Cameroons. Trade continued in the same way, however, with the Duala as middlemen and with slaves as the main cargo. Then in 1807, England outlawed the slave trade. Historians estimate that during the period of the slave trade about seven hundred people a year from Cameroon were sold into slavery. Cash crops, such as palm oil and palm kernels, ivory, and rubber, replaced slaves as items of trade. Farmers in Cameroon expanded the land used for growing crops.

By the mid-1800s, the British had worked out treaties with Duala chiefs. British traders established headquarters on land in Cameroon. They were followed by English Baptist missionaries who built schools and churches. In 1858, a British missionary founded the town of Victoria, now called Limbe. During the same time, French and German traders also set up posts along the coast. Between the 1830s and 1880s, Duala chiefs frequently asked to be taken under the British government's protection. They thought they would receive better treatment from the British. Britain wasn't interested, though.

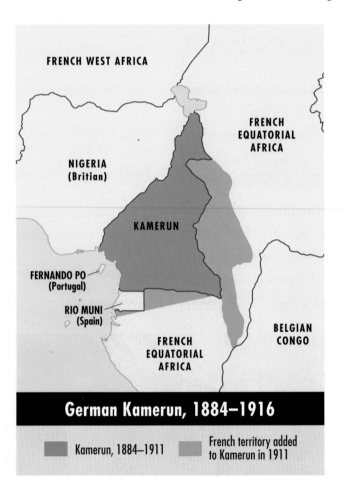

German Kamerun, 1884–1916

Kamerun, 1884–1911

French territory added to Kamerun in 1911

The German Protectorate of Kamerun

In the 1870s and 1880s, Britain, France, Spain, and Germany were beginning to stake out territories in Africa. This was known as the Great Race for Africa. At the Berlin Conference

(1884–1885) in Germany, these nations made an agreement about lands in Africa. They agreed that any country wishing ownership over a part of Africa had to have government representatives there.

The Berlin Conference was made up of representatives from European countries who discussed territorial claims in Africa.

In July 1884, before the Berlin Conference, Gustav Nachtigal, a German explorer and government representative, signed a treaty with two Duala chiefs. As a result, Cameroon became the German Protectorate of Kamerun. According to the treaty, Germany's control was limited to the coast. In 1885, however, German explorers pushed farther inland. Although they sometimes met with resistance, they made treaties and formed relationships with chiefs of other ethnic groups. By 1911, Germany had control of Cameroon from the seacoast to Lake Chad.

Doctor turned explorer, Gustav Nachtigal, aided Germany in claiming Cameroon as a German Protectorate.

Under German control, many changes came to Cameroon. Inland in the southwest, land was cleared for big plantations. Large cash crops of coffee, tea, cocoa, palm oil, and bananas were grown. Ports were developed at Douala and other coastal towns so that large ships could enter easily. Wharves and warehouses were built at the ports to hold goods before shipment. Roads were cut that linked

While Cameroon was a protectorate of Germany, local people were put to work building railway lines.

most parts of Cameroon. Bridges were built over rivers. In 1890, Yaoundé was founded as a military post. From Douala, the Germans constructed a railroad that went west to Nkongsamba and east to Yaoundé.

The people of Cameroon were also affected by German rule. Most of the workers who built the plantations, roads, and railroads were forced laborers who were moved from their home areas. Many became ill or died. They weren't used to the food, weather, or diseases in the work areas. In addition, the churches and schools built by the British were closed. In the 1880s, German Baptist and Catholic missionaries set up new churches and schools where the German language was taught. Although the slave trade had ended in the early 1800s, various people in Cameroon, especially the Fulani, still used slaves. In 1902, Germany outlawed slavery in Cameroon.

In 1914 World War I broke out in Europe. France and Britain fought Germany. The war spread to Africa. At that time, Britain controlled Nigeria, to the west of Cameroon. France controlled all the land east and south of Cameroon,

During World War I, Cameroon was taken by Britain and France. Here, soldiers practice field artillery.

An Early Nationalist

Douala Rudolf Manga Bell (1873–1914) was the son of the Duala chief who signed the treaty that created the German Protectorate of Kamerun. Born in Douala, Manga Bell was educated in Cameroon and in Germany. In 1910, he succeeded his father as king. Manga Bell attacked the German treatment of Cameroon and its people. Because of his outspokenness, he was arrested and condemned to death. In August 1914, shortly after World War I broke out, he was hanged. Only in recent years has he been honored by the Cameroon government. Manga Bell is one of Cameroon's national heroes.

except for Spanish land that now is Equatorial Guinea. In 1914, Britain and France invaded Cameroon. By 1916, they had defeated the Germans and divided the former Kamerun between them.

British Cameroons and French Cameroun

As a result of World War I, Britain and France controlled Cameroon. Britain had control of the western one-fifth from the Alantika Mountains to the coast. Britain's area was further divided into Northern Cameroons and Southern Cameroons. The rest of Cameroon became French Cameroun. In 1922, British Cameroons and French Cameroun were recognized by the League of Nations as mandates. As such, Britain and France were expected to set up responsible governments and to end the abuses that had taken place during the German colonial period.

British Cameroons was governed as part of Nigeria, a British colony. Britain used a policy of indirect rule in Cameroon. Local leaders, such as fons and lamidos, were appointed to collect taxes, keep up the roads, take care of

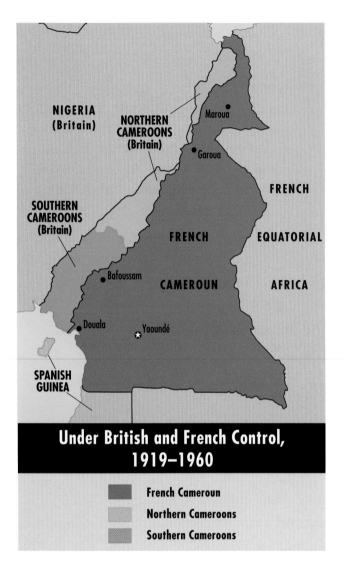

Under British and French Control, 1919–1960

NIGERIA (Britain)

NORTHERN CAMEROONS (Britain)

Maroua

Garoua

FRENCH

SOUTHERN CAMEROONS (Britain)

FRENCH

EQUATORIAL

Bafoussam

CAMEROUN

AFRICA

Douala

Yaoundé

SPANISH GUINEA

French Cameroun
Northern Cameroons
Southern Cameroons

their people's health, and make judgments regarding minor crimes. In return, the local leaders could keep half the money they collected. Because the British weren't interested in taking over the former German plantations, German landowners were permitted to buy them back. German missionaries were allowed to return. Many Nigerians moved into British Cameroon. Some became landowners; others worked in the towns. The British built schools for the Cameroonians. Although English was the official language, African languages were used to teach children in the primary schools. English language instruction came later. All in all, the main British policy was to help the Cameroonians to live as Africans.

The French, on the other hand, governed French Cameroun as another French colony. Their goal was to have the Cameroonians put aside their traditional society and culture and accept French values and culture. In other words, they were to become French citizens and part of the French nation. For Cameroonians to become French citizens, they had to speak French, be willing to serve in the French army, and have a Western profession, such as teacher, lawyer, scientist, or government official. The rest of the Cameroonians were considered subjects with limited civil rights. The French also continued the use of forced labor for road building and work on plantations. By the late 1930s, though, some improvements had occurred in French Cameroun. Missionaries operated primary schools throughout the colony. The French government supported secondary and technical schools and built hospitals in some larger towns.

From 1939 to 1945, during World War II, Britain and France again fought Germany. In British Cameroons, the Germans were once more forced to leave. In French Cameroun, Cameroonians served in the French army. In both British Cameroons and French Cameroun, production of cash crops was increased for export to help the war effort. World War II ended with another German defeat.

Toward Independence and Reunification

After World War II, the United Nations replaced the League of Nations. Under the United Nations, the two Cameroons' status was changed from mandates to trusteeships. As such, they were eventually to achieve self-government and independence. However, neither Britain nor France was eager to free its colonies. Instead, France allowed French Cameroun to send representatives to the French National Assembly in Paris. An elected territorial assembly was also formed in French Cameroun, and Cameroonians could begin to form political parties. In British Cameroons, Britain set up a House of Assembly.

Nevertheless, anticolonial feelings in both parts of Cameroon led to the rise of nationalist groups. In British Cameroons, the nationalists were brought into the colonial governing body. The French, however, tried to crush the nationalists. This led to an anticolonial uprising (1955–1957) waged by members of the Union of Cameroonian People (UCP) against French and colonial troops. The UCP, formed in 1948 by Reuben Um Nyobe (1913–1958), called for an end to French rule and reunification with British Cameroons. In 1955, the Kamerun National Democratic Party (KNDP) was formed in British Cameroons. It called for separation from Nigeria and union with French Cameroun.

From 1955 to 1959, the French government gradually moved toward self-government for French Cameroun. In 1958, the Legislative Assembly of Cameroun voted for independence by 1960. In 1959 French Cameroun was given full self-government. Ahmadou Ahidjo became prime minister of French Cameroun. Also in 1959, John Foncha, the founder of the KNDP, became prime minister in British Cameroons. The two leaders talked about unification.

In 1960, French Cameroun became the Independent Republic of Cameroun. A new National Assembly was elected, and Ahidjo was elected as the republic's first president. In 1961, the people in British Cameroons voted on whether

In 1960, Cameroon's Ahmadou Ahidjo (second from left) celebrated independence with France's minister of state Louis Jacquinot (left).

to stay in or leave Nigeria. Those in Northern British Cameroons voted to stay in Nigeria. Those in Southern British Cameroons voted to leave and to join the Republic of Cameroun. With that vote, the Federal Republic of Cameroon came into being. Ahidjo became president; Foncha, vice president.

From Federal Republic to Republic of Cameroon

Under the federal republic, Cameroon had two states: a large French-speaking East Cameroon and a much smaller English-speaking West Cameroon. Each state had its own prime minister and legislature. In addition, there was a Federal National Assembly whose representatives were chosen by the state legislatures. Direct elections of the Federal National Assembly took place in 1964. Ahmadou Ahidjo was reelected as president in 1965. His party, the Cameroon Union (UC), was the only legal party in East Cameroon. The KNDP was the official party in West Cameroon.

Civil war activities between the UCP and the government continued for several more years. The Bamiléké, Bassa, and Duala were active groups within the UCP. Putting down rebellions cost the new government heavily in money and troops.

During the 1960s, Ahidjo worked to unify the people of Cameroon and the two states of Cameroon. He centralized all parts of the government in the capital at Yaoundé. He placed people from all major ethnic groups, both French-speaking and English-speaking, in government positions. The government became the main source of funds for developing the

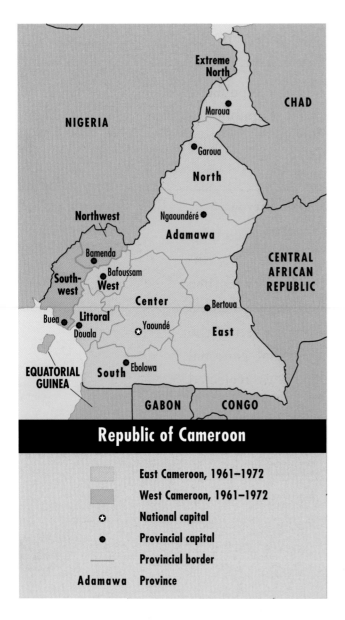

Republic of Cameroon

East Cameroon, 1961–1972
West Cameroon, 1961–1972
⊙ National capital
● Provincial capital
— Provincial border
Adamawa Province

country. It actually owned much land and many industries. In 1966, Ahidjo merged the UC and KNDP into the Cameroon National Union (CNU), which he controlled. Nevertheless, people and groups who opposed Ahidjo were dealt with harshly. Freedom of speech and of the press were limited by government censorship and arrests.

In 1972, Ahidjo felt that the country was unified. He called for elections to replace the federal republic with a unitary or united republic. Ahidjo remained as president in complete control of Cameroon. At that time, Cameroon had seven provinces. In 1975, Ahidjo created the position of prime minister and appointed Paul Biya to it. Three years later, Ahidjo made the prime minister the successor to the president. Then, in 1982, Ahidjo actually turned the presidency over to Biya. Ahidjo had thought he would keep his power and work in the background. Paul Biya put his own people into government positions, however, and began to move toward a more democratic state. He also added three provinces by dividing the Northern and the Center South provinces. Ahidjo, who was living in France, tried to overthrow Biya's government in 1983 and again in 1984. Biya had Ahidjo condemned to death and ordered about one hundred of the rebels executed.

Later in 1984, Biya declared the Republic of Cameroon to be the official name of the country. In 1985, he changed the name of the CNU to Cameroon People's Democratic Movement (CPDM). In French, this is the *Rassemblement Démocratique du Peuple Camerounais* (RDPC). Although Biya promoted democratic changes, the only legal political party was the CPDM. Biya also set limits on freedom of the press. Finally, in 1990, other political parties were allowed and multiparty elections were held.

During the 1990s, several disputes between ethnic groups flared up. Biya's police quickly stopped them. In December 1999, anglophones, English-speaking people, led a movement to have what once was West Cameroon leave the republic. They claimed that English speakers were discriminated against. Biya also had this movement put down. Thus, Paul Biya maintained strong control over the government and of Cameroon into the early 2000s.

Cameroon's Changing Status	
German Protectorate of Kamerun	1884–1916
Occupation by British and French	1916–1919
French Cameroun and British Cameroons	1919–1922
League of Nation Mandates: French Cameroun, British Cameroons	1922–1946
United Nations Trust Territories: French Cameroun, British Cameroons	1946–1960
Independent Republic of Cameroun (Former French Cameroun)	1960–1961
Federal Republic of Cameroon (Union with Southern British Cameroons)	1961–1972
United Republic of Cameroon	1972–1984
Republic of Cameroon	1984–present

A Stable Government

SINCE GAINING INDEPENDENCE IN 1960, CAMEROON HAS maintained a reputation for a stable government. Nevertheless, Cameroon has experienced fighting among ethnic groups and an attempt by anglophones to secede from the country. However, these incidents are considered minor when compared with the bloody civil wars that continue to take place in neighboring countries. The fact that President Ahidjo voluntarily stepped down from office before the end of his term was also remarkable for an African government. When he later tried to overthrow President Biya, his motives were strongly questioned.

Much of Cameroon's seeming stability, however, rests on another reality, that of a corrupt dictatorship. In 1998 and 1999, the organization Transparency International ranked Cameroon as the most corrupt country in the world. By 2002 it had moved up to thirteenth from the bottom in this world ranking. If something is transparent, it can be seen through. If a nation is transparent, it is open and honest with nothing to hide. Cameroon's government still operates in an environment of fraud, corruption, bribery, and violent abuse. Human and civil rights guaranteed by Cameroon's constitution are often violated. Cameroonians' access to information through newspapers, radio, television, and the Internet is limited. All these factors make Cameroon lacking in transparency.

In 1996, a new constitution was adopted. The term of the presidency was lengthened from five years to seven years.

A schoolchild carries the flag of Cameroon during one of the country's public holidays.

However, a person now cannot be elected more than twice to that office. A Senate was added to the legislative branch. The constitution also reaffirms that the capital is Yaoundé, describes the country's flag, and states what the national anthem and national motto are. Cameroon's motto is "Work, Peace, Fatherland."

Cameroon's Flag

From left to right, Cameroon's national flag has three equal vertical bands of color: green, red, and yellow. Each color stands for one of Cameroon's major geographic areas: green for the rain forest, red for the soil of the savanna, and yellow for the dry northern land. The yellow star in the center of the red band represents the unity of the Republic of Cameroon.

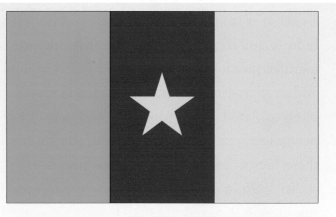

Cameroon's National Anthem

The music and French words of Cameroon's national anthem were written in 1928. Gradually the song began to represent the Cameroonian desire for independence. In 1960, the song was officially declared to be the national anthem of the Republic of Cameroon. The national anthem's title is *O Cameroun, Berceau de Nos Ancêtres* ("O Cameroon, Cradle of Our Fathers"). The English words are not a translation of the French.

French Version of the National Anthem

O Cameroun berceau de nos ancêtres,
va, debout, et jaloux de ta liberté,
comme un soleil, ton drapeau fier doit être,
un symbole ardent de foi et d'unité.

Chorus:
Chère Patrie, Terre chérie,
Tu es notre seul et vrai bonheur,
Notre joie et notre vie,
A toi l'amour et le grand honneur.
Que tous tes entants du Nord et Sud,
De l'Est à l'Ouest soit tout amour,
Te servir que ce soit le seul but,
Pour remplir leur devoir toujours.

English Version of the Cameroon National Anthem

O Cameroon, Thou Cradle of our Fathers.
Holy Shrine where in our midst they now repose,
Their tears and blood and sweat thy soil did water,
On thy hills and valleys once their tillage rose.
Dear Fatherland, thy worth no tongue can tell!
How can we ever pay thy due?
Thy welfare we will win in toil and love and peace,
Will be to thy name ever true!

Chorus:
Land of Promise, land of Glory!
Thou, of life and joy, our only store!
Thine be honor, thine devotion
and deep endearment, for evermore.
From Shari, from where the Mungo meanders
From along the banks of lowly Boumba Stream,
Muster thy sons in union close around thee,
Mighty as the Buéa Mountain be their team;
Instill in them the love of gentle ways,
Regret for errors of the past;
Foster, for Mother Africa, a loyalty
That true shall remain to the last.

The Executive Branch of Government

The president is the head of the executive branch, as well as the head of state. The president must be born in Cameroon and be at least thirty-five years old. The president is directly elected by all voters in the entire nation. According to the new constitution, the term of office is seven years, and the

Cameroon's Presidential Palace

president can be reelected only once. President Biya has been elected once under the new constitution, in 1997, but he had already been in office since 1982. He will be up for reelection in 2004. Cameroon's presidents live in the Unity Palace, also called the Presidential Palace, their official residence in Yaoundé.

The president holds most of the political and governmental power in Cameroon. He appoints the prime minister and has approval of all the ministers in the Council of Ministers. There are almost thirty ministries that take care of everything in the country from agriculture to youth and sports. The president also decides what the ministers do and how long they may do it. Since 1975, several women have been appointed ministers. In that year, Delphine Zanga Tsogo Tsang became the minister of social affairs. The president also appoints judges to the Supreme Court and names ambassadors to other countries. One of the president's main powers is enacting laws passed by Parliament. Most of the laws are already part of the president's program, which the legislature is supposed to approve. Other presidential powers include declaring a state of emergency for internal problems and declaring a state of war for external problems. To help him carry out his war-making power, Cameroon's president is also head of the armed forces.

Cameroon's Two Presidents

Ahmadou Ahidjo (below) (1924–1989) was Cameroon's first president, elected in 1960 and reelected in 1965, 1970, 1975, and 1980. He was born in Garoua, North Province, into a Fulani Muslim family. Ahidjo attended primary school in Garoua and secondary school in Yaoundé. Before becoming involved in politics, he worked as a radio operator for the Posts and Telegraph Service in Douala. Under French rule, he worked his way up from a delegate in the Territorial Assembly to prime minister. Becoming president in 1960, he soon gathered all political power to himself. During his years in power, Cameroon's economy grew but the people's rights were limited. After unsuccessfully trying to overthrow his hand-picked successor in 1983 and 1984, he spent the rest of his life in exile in France and Senegal. In 1989, he died in Dakar, Senegal.

In 1982, Ahidjo turned the presidency over to Paul Biya (above) (1933–). Biya was born into a Christian Beti family in Mvomeka'a, South Province. He attended primary and secondary schools in Cameroon. In Paris, France, he graduated from college and from law school. When he returned to Cameroon, it had become an independent country. Receiving a government position in President Ahidjo's office in 1962, Biya remained close to Ahidjo until 1983. By that time, Biya had been named president and Ahidjo tried to overthrow him. During Biya's presidency, Cameroon's economy has suffered and there have been many political problems. However, Biya continues to hold the presidency, with the next election to be held in 2004, the last in which he will be eligible to run.

Yaoundé: Did You Know This?

Built among a jumble of hills and ravines in Cameroon's Center Province, Yaoundé stands about 2,460 feet (750 m) above sea level. Residents enjoy year-round temperatures of about 75°F (24°C). Annual rainfall is about 62 inches (157 cm). In 1888, German explorer Georg August Zenker founded the city as a German administrative, military, and trading post. Under the French mandate and trusteeship, Yaoundé became the capital of French Cameroun. Today, Cameroon's elected representatives meet in Yaoundé; conferences are held in the Palais des Congrès; and about forty countries from around the world have embassies throughout the city. The University of Yaoundé is the city's main center of learning. The National Museum and the Afhemi Museum exhibit Cameroonian works of art and crafts. Northwest of

the city is a Benedictine monastery that houses the Museum of Cameroonian Art. To the south is Unity Palace, where the president lives. Yaoundé is in the Ewondo ethnic group's territory, but large numbers of people from other ethnic groups, such as the Fulani, Bamiléké, and Beti, also now live in the city. The capital's 2003 population was about 1,200,000.

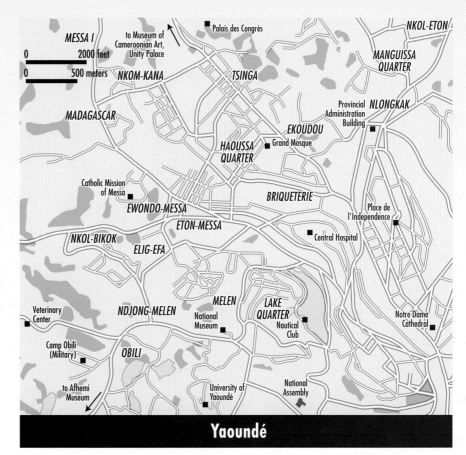

Yaoundé

The Legislative Branch

According to the 1996 constitution, Cameroon's legislature changed from one house to two houses. A Senate was added to the National Assembly. However, Senate elections have not yet been held. The National Assembly is made up of 180 members. They are elected for a five-year term. They represent all the people of Cameroon. In other words, they do not represent districts as is the case with the U.S. House of Representatives. In the 2002 election, sixteen women were elected to the assembly. That's about 9 percent of the members.

NATIONAL GOVERNMENT OF CAMEROON

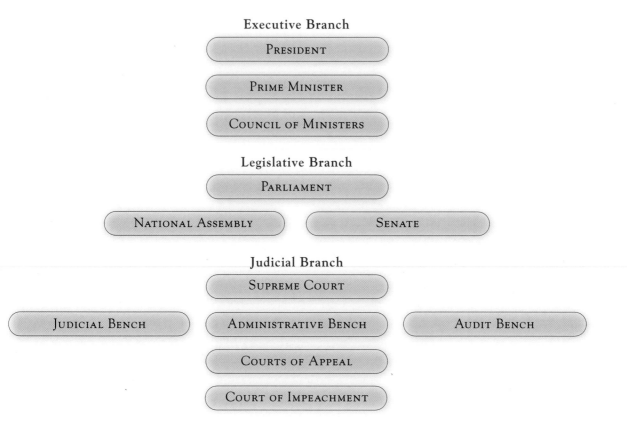

Executive Branch

- PRESIDENT
- PRIME MINISTER
- COUNCIL OF MINISTERS

Legislative Branch

- PARLIAMENT
- NATIONAL ASSEMBLY
- SENATE

Judicial Branch

- SUPREME COURT
- JUDICIAL BENCH
- ADMINISTRATIVE BENCH
- AUDIT BENCH
- COURTS OF APPEAL
- COURT OF IMPEACHMENT

One duty of the assembly is to pass the budget presented by the president. Other duties include passing laws that protect citizens' rights, that regulate land ownership, social security, and insurance, and that regulate trade unions, political parties, and the school system. Currently, the National Assembly meets in March, June, and November of each year. The president can call an end to a session of the assembly and can call for new elections.

When the Senate is organized, it will have one hundred senators who will represent the provinces. Seventy senators will be elected, and thirty will be appointed by the president. Their terms will also be for five years. Their duties will be the same as those of members of the National Assembly. Senators, however, will not be involved with passing the budget.

Judicial Branch

The Supreme Court is the highest court in Cameroon. It has a president and nine judges and is made up of three benches. The judicial bench makes rulings on appeals from lower courts. The administrative bench makes decisions on election disputes. The audit bench makes rulings on financial matters, such as government or business accounts.

Another important court is the Court of Impeachment. This court has the power to try the president for treason and to try the prime minister and any government officials who might conspire against the government.

In northern Cameroon, a government official addresses a crowd.

Local Government

According to the new constitution, Cameroon's provinces are now called regions. They are supposed to have an elected regional president and regional council. However, these elections have not taken place. Instead, the regions are each still headed by a governor whom President Biya appoints.

The regions are divided into divisions, subdivisions, and districts. All these layers of regional government are controlled by officials appointed by the government in Yaoundé.

Unofficial local government continues in the form of the fons, lamidos, and other traditional chiefs. These chiefs and leaders regulate day-to-day affairs in their villages and towns. They also hand down judgments in civil suits, such as landownership issues. Criminal suits are handled by the provincial governments. The local leaders receive small salaries from the central government.

Cameroonians hold on to their culture with unofficial local government officials. This is Hapi IV, king of the Bana tribe.

Cameroon's cities, however, do have official local governments in the form of councils. In 2002, several political parties ran candidates for 336 city council seats across the country. The RDPC won 286 of those seats.

Political Parties, Elections, and Voting

Until 1990, there had been only one legal party, the RDPC. President Biya continues to be the head of this party. By 2002 Cameroon had 159 legal political parties. The most powerful opposition party is the Social Democratic Front (SDF). Its leader is John Fru Ndi, a businessman from Bamenda. In 1992, he ran for president against Biya. It is believed that Fru Ndi won the election, but Biya claimed the victory and placed Fru Ndi under house arrest. International observers declared that there were great flaws in the election process. Because of fraud and abuse during the 1992 election, John Fru Ndi and the SDF refused to take part in the 1997 presidential election. At least six candidates did oppose Biya in 1997. However, he won with 92 percent of the vote.

In the 2002 National Assembly election, the RDPC won 149 of the 180 seats. The SDF came in second with twenty-two seats. The remaining nine seats were split among three other political parties. With such a large majority, President Biya's party has no problem passing laws favored by the president.

Foreign Relations

Since independence, Cameroon has maintained close relationships with France, Britain, and the United States. Ties

with France continue to be especially strong through trade and financial aid. In 2000, Cameroon received U.S.$44 million in aid from France. Cultural ties with France remain strong, and Cameroon is a full-time member of the "Francophone," an organization of French-speaking states. Each year a Franco-African summit is held in Paris, France, to discuss common concerns. The program for the 2003 meeting was planned in Cameroon. In 1995, Britain admitted Cameroon into the Commonwealth. For a while, this improved the relationship of Cameroon's anglophones with the government in Yaoundé. Each year Cameroon receives about U.S.$5 million

At the 2001 Franco-African Summit, a Cameroonian girl presents France's president Jacques Chirac with flowers.

Representatives and leaders of African countries come to Paris, France, each year to attend the Franco-African Summit in hope of continuing a partnership with France.

in aid from the United States that is used for health and education programs. More than one hundred U.S. Peace Corps volunteers work in Cameroon. They train teachers, set up medical clinics, provide information about HIV/AIDS, explain more efficient farming methods, and demonstrate ways to improve the environment—especially in the rain forest.

Cameroon has been a member of the United Nations since 1960. In December 2000, the country was elected to serve a two-year term (2001–2003) on the Security Council. In early 2003, Cameroon took part in debates on resolutions regarding disarming Iraq. These debates involved whether to support the United States' plan to go to war against Iraq if it did not disarm. Cameroon preferred to avoid war and to keep on with weapons' inspections in Iraq. If Iraq continued to be uncooperative, Cameroon seemed to be ready to back the United States but chose to abstain in the final vote.

Within Africa, Cameroon has generally had good relations with its neighbors and belongs to several African organizations. Since the early 1990s, however, Cameroon and Nigeria have carried on a dispute over ownership of the oil-rich Bakassi Peninsula. Nigeria occupied the area in 1993. Since then, sporadic fighting has broken out between the Nigerian and Cameroonian armies. In 2002, the International Court of Justice declared that the peninsula belonged to Cameroon, but Nigeria rejected the ruling. Since then, the two countries have formed a Joint Border Commission to resolve the issue. In 2003, in another dispute, Nigeria agreed to transfer thirty-three villages near Lake Chad to Cameroon ownership.

Working for a Prosperous Economy

As Cameroon's wealth increases, funds are put to good use, such as paving roads for instance.

C

AMEROON'S CASH CROPS OF COCOA, COFFEE, AND COTton; the logging industry; and rich oil deposits together form the basis of the country's economy. From the 1960s into the 1980s, these products made Cameroon one of West Africa's wealthiest nations. It was also one of the few African countries that grew enough food to feed itself. Under these conditions, Cameroon's government obtained loans from other countries. Money from the loans paid for a great building program. The railroad was extended from Yaoundé to Ngaoundéré. Roads were paved, and new roads were cut. Schools and hospitals went up throughout the country. During these busy years many industries were owned or closely managed by the government.

Opposite: **Coffee crops contribute to Cameroon's economic strength, which continues steadily to grow.**

Cameroon's Currency

Cameroon belongs to the Central African Financial Community (CFAF), along with the country's five Central African neighbors. This group's currency is called the CFA franc. Once tied to the French franc, the CFA franc now is pegged to the euro: 1 euro equals 677 CFA francs. In U.S. dollars, 618 CFA francs equal $1.00. The French treasury guarantees the CFA franc.

Each of the six countries prints and mints its own currency, and each honors the currency of the other five. Coins in CFA francs come in the following denominations: 1, 5, 10, 25, 50, 100, and 250 francs. Paper currency is issued in 500, 1,000, 2,000, 5,000, and 10,000 franc notes.

Cameroon's paper currency is colorful and informative. One note has pictures of antelopes on the savanna. Other notes depict Cameroon's cotton, cocoa, coffee, or banana crops. Still others highlight the country's fishing, logging, shipping, and oil industries.

In the mid-1980s, worldwide prices for oil, cotton, cocoa, and coffee dropped. Interest rates went up for loans. The government fell deeply into debt and could not repay its loans. Cameroon's economy and its people suffered greatly. By the late 1980s, the government had begun reforms. The World Bank and the International Monetary Fund had worked out agreements for Cameroon's debt relief. The government had to make many reforms, though, to qualify for this relief. The salaries of government workers were reduced. Cameroon's state industries were to become privately owned.

By 2002, most of the government-owned industries were in private hands. Since the foreign debt is at U.S.$8.6 billion and the average per capita income is only about U.S.$600, much still needs to be done. By 2003, however, Cameroon was showing a steady economic growth of 5 percent a year.

What a CFA Franc Buys in Cameroon

Item	Cost in CFA Francs	Cost in U.S.$
1 banana	10 CFA	$0.02
1 pound (0.45 kilogram) cheese	3,000 CFA	$4.85
1 pound (0.45 kilogram) meat	600 CFA	$0.97
Ice cream cone	150 CFA	$0.24
1 gallon (3.8 liters) gasoline	2,200 CFA	$3.56
Barbie doll	12,000 CFA	$19.42
Soccer ball	5,000 CFA	$8.09

Farming, Fishing, and Forestry

About 75 percent of Cameroon's workers are engaged in farming, fishing, or forestry. Farmers make up most of this group. They grow the country's cash crops that are exported or used in Cameroon's industries. In the north, cotton is the main cash crop. Arabica coffee is grown in the west; robusta coffee flourishes in the southern rain forest. Cocoa, tea, bananas, and oil palm trees flourish in the south. Sugarcane does well in the south, too. Farmers also grow the food crops for Cameroonians. In the north, they harvest groundnuts, millet, and cassava. Rice is grown in flooded areas of the northeast and in the west. Cassava is an important crop in the south, along with beans, sweet potatoes, yams,

An abundant cotton crop will provide Cameroon's farmers with a good income.

Above left: **Fishing is not a large industry in Cameroon. Here, local boys scoop fish with a net.**

Above right: **Cameroon has a wealth of trees. Environmentalists hope that the logging industry will decrease their production to preserve the rain forest.**

maize (corn), and beans. Individual farmers herd cattle, sheep, goats, and pigs. Chickens are mainly raised on commercial farms.

Fishing makes up a small percentage of Cameroon's economy. Fishers along Cameroon's rivers and at the coast supply local needs only. Forestry, however, is one of Cameroon's big money makers. The rain forests have about three hundred kinds of trees with commercial value. Logs from these trees bring in about U.S.$120 million a year. Although efforts are being made to decrease logging because of environmental interests, Cameroon's rain forest is disappearing at a rate of about 0.6 percent a year.

What Cameroon Grows, Makes, and Mines

Agriculture (1999 est.)

Cassava	1,500,000 metric tons
Sugarcane	1,350,000 metric tons
Plantains	1,000,000 metric tons

Manufacturing (in CFA Francs; 1994 est.)

Beverages	49,314,000
Wood and wood products	42,756,000
Rubber and plastic products	38,928,000

Mining

Oil (2001 est.)	4,000,000 metric tons
Pozzolana	100,000 metric tons
Bauxite (1996 est.)	82,000 metric tons
Limestone (1996 est.)	50,000 metric tons

Mining and Power Resources

In 1976, Cameroon's first oil well was drilled off the northwest coast. Since then, oil has been found near the Logone River in the north and near Mamfé in the west. In addition, the Bakassi Peninsula is thought to be rich in oil because it is between oil fields in Cameroon and Nigeria. Oil production reached its highest point in 1985 at 158,000 barrels per day. In 2001, only 77,000 barrels per day were pumped. Not including possible oil on the peninsula, Cameroon's oil fields have only about 330 million barrels left. Engineers think these reserves will be gone within ten to twenty years. In the meantime, Cameroon will make money from the construction of the Chad-Cameroon Pipeline. This 650-mile (1,046-km) pipeline

Workers inspect pipes that will be used to build the Chad-Cameroon Pipeline.

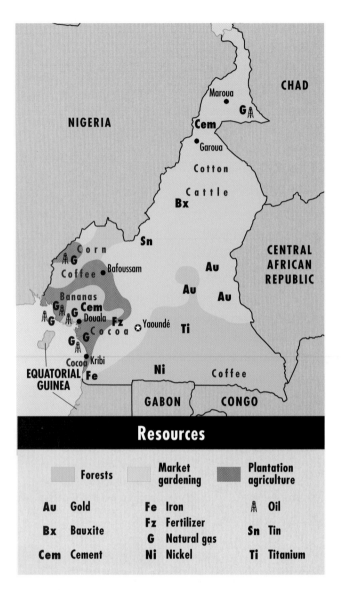

Resources

Forests	Market gardening	Plantation agriculture

Au	Gold	Fe	Iron	⚒	Oil
Bx	Bauxite	Fz	Fertilizer	Sn	Tin
		G	Natural gas	Ti	Titanium
Cem	Cement	Ni	Nickel		

was completed by the end of 2003. It carries oil from southern Chad to the port of Kribi in Cameroon.

Cameroon is rich in other mineral resources as well, but little has been done to develop them. Natural gas deposits have been found near the oil fields and offshore near the mouth of the Sanaga River. Iron ore remains undeveloped near Kribi. Large bauxite deposits, from which aluminum is made, are in the west near Minim Martap and Ngoundal. Limestone, quarried near Garoua, is used to make cement. Pozzolana, another stone used in making cement, is also found in Cameroon.

Cameroon's rivers are a source of hydroelectric power. In the south, on the Sanaga River, power plants have been built at Edéa and Song-Loulou. A plant on the Bénué River supplies power to the north. Hydroelectric power supplies about 98 percent of the country's electricity. Cameroon's industries use most of this power, with the aluminum plant at Edéa taking about 50 percent of it. The rest of the power runs mainly to the cities of Yaoundé, Douala, and Bafoussam. Most of the rest of the country has no electricity or is served by diesel-generated electricity.

Manufacturing

Most of Cameroon's industries are based on processing raw materials. Limbe has an oil refinery; Edéa, an aluminum plant; Douala and Garoua, cement plants. Since fewer logs are exported now, wood processing has become a big business. Several sawmills, lumber mills, and plywood factories have opened. Some textile mills make thread and cloth from cotton. A factory makes cotton oil.

Food processing is another important industry. Products include chocolate, cocoa paste, soft drinks, fruit drinks, peanut oil, palm oil, sugar, and flour. Other industries produce furniture, leather, shoes, tires, and soap.

Service Industries

Transportation, trade, banking, and tourism are major service industries in Cameroon. Although there are about 30,635 miles (49,300 km) of roads, only 2,548 miles (4,100 km) are paved. Most roads are impassable in the rainy season and choked with dust in the dry season. Because its road and rail services are weak, the country is striving to improve them. Since 2002, plans were also being made to extend the railroad from Douala to Grand Batanga,

During the rainy season, local cars and trucks have a difficult time passing through washed out and muddy roads.

In the port at Douala, cargo ships import and export goods.

just south of Kribi. Another rail line is being planned from Kribi to the Central African Republic. Cameroon has international airports at Douala, Yaoundé, and Garoua, and domestic airports at smaller cities. Cameroon Airlines makes stops throughout Cameroon, as well as in other African countries and Europe.

Most trade is handled at the main seaport of Douala. The port at Kribi handles wood and mineral products; the one at Limbe, oil. Cameroon's main exports are oil, timber, cocoa, and coffee. Most of these goods go to Italy, Spain, and France. The value of exports equals about U.S.$2 billion a year. Manufactured goods and fuel are Cameroon's main imports. They come mainly from France, Nigeria, and Italy. The cost of these imports is about U.S.$1.6 billion a year.

Banking is another important service industry in Cameroon. The economic troubles of the late 1980s caused many banks to close. By the late 1990s, though, several new banks had opened, including Citicorp of Cameroon. Other banks are under French management. With the help of Canada, a system of community banks called micro banks has started in rural areas. Individuals deposit savings and can take out loans. Most of the loans are used to improve farming practices and increase crop production. Cameroonian women have gained a larger voice in community affairs by taking part

System of Weights and Measures

Cameroon uses the metric system.

in the micro-banking system. A less formal banking system also takes place in villages and neighborhoods in cities. Each week a group of workers contributes a set amount of their wages. The workers take turns receiving this large amount of money. It is most often used for a major expense, such as repairs to a house.

Tourism offers Cameroon a way to increase its income. In the late 1990s, Cameroon had about 135,000 tourists, who spent around U.S.$40 million each year. By 2004, the Tourism Ministry plans to attract 500,000 international visitors to Cameroon. Part of the plan calls for a tourism office in the United States. The Tourism Ministry uses the slogan "Africa in Miniature." This emphasizes the variety of tourist attrac-

Tourism is on the rise in Cameroon. Here, tourists journeyed through the rain forest to the falls at Kribi.

tions, such as beaches, national parks, savanna safaris, a volcanic mountain, cities, and ethnic villages. Cameroon also has active tourism within the country. Limbe's beaches attract people from Douala on weekends and holidays. Beaches at Kribi are a popular getaway spot for government officials. A wide range of hotels, guest houses, and restaurants are in place to serve Cameroon's visitors.

Many Ethnic Groups and Languages

I N 2002, CAMEROON HAD AN ESTIMATED POPULATION OF 16 million people. That's about the number of people who live in the state of Florida. Cameroon is still mainly a rural coun-try. About half of Cameroonians live in villages. The number of people who live in cities, however, has increased from 39 per-cent in 1990 to 50 percent in 2003. Cameroon is also a very young country. About 42 percent of the people are under fifteen years of age. In the United States, only 21 percent of the people are in this age group.

The population density is about eighty-seven Cameroonians per square mile (thirty-four per sq km). This is about the same population density as the state of Alabama. Cameroonians, however, are not spread out evenly throughout the

Opposite: **Cameroonians are a varied people made up of more than two hun-dred different ethnic groups.**

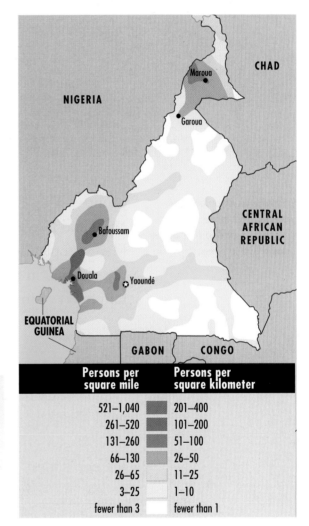

Population of Major Cities		
Douala	1,320,000	(1995)
Yaoundé	1,120,000	(1999)
Garoua	160,000	(1992)
Maroua	140,000	(1992)
Bafoussam	120,000	(1992)

Persons per square mile	Persons per square kilometer
521–1,040	201–400
261–520	101–200
131–260	51–100
66–130	26–50
26–65	11–25
3–25	1–10
fewer than 3	fewer than 1

Cameroon's population is wide spread throughout its villages. Only one-half of the people live in cities.

country. The largest number of people live in the western cities and large villages of the grasslands and along the coast. Many people also live in the south-central rain forest and on the savanna in the mid-north. Few people live in the eastern rain forest or in parts of the far north.

The People of Cameroon

Although the people of Cameroon are all called Cameroonians, they also consider themselves members of more than two hundred ethnic groups and subgroups. The three largest ethnic clusters account for more than one-half of the population. Based on language, the three main groups of people in Cameroon are the Bantu, the semi-Bantu, and the Sudanese. People who belong to Bantu ethnic groups include the Duala, Luanda, and Basa. These Bantu peoples live in cities and villages along the coast. Another Bantu group is the Fang, which is further divided into the Beti, Eton, Ewondo, and many other groups. The Fang people live mainly in cities and villages in the southern forests and are also the dominant ethnic group in Gabon and Equatorial Guinea. Semi-Bantu people include the Bamiléké, Bamoun, and Tikar. Their cities

Bamoun women stand outside their hut.

Fulani men

Bamiléké boys dance in a traditional initiation ceremony.

and villages are in the western grasslands between the Adamawa Plateau and the Cameroon Mountains. The Fulani are the major Sudanese ethnic group. They live north of the Adamawa Plateau.

The Bamiléké are Cameroon's largest single ethnic group. Because of their numbers and of the small size of their homeland, many have moved from the grasslands to cities throughout the country. The Bamiléké have become

Major Ethnic Groups in Cameroon (1983 est.)	
Fang (Beti, BLU, Eton, Ewondo, etc.)	19.6%
Bamiléké, Bamoun	18.5%
Duala, Luanda, Basa	14.7%
Fulani	9.6%
Tikar	7.4%
Mandara	5.7%
Maka	4.9%
Chamba	2.4%
Mbum	1.3%
Hausa	1.2%
French	0.2%
All others (Cameroonians, Africans, Europeans, Americans, etc.)	14.5%

successful businesspeople wherever they live. Their success has caused jealousy among non-Bamilékés and has led to riots and bloodshed several times since the 1960s. The Bamiléké themselves feel discriminated against by the government. Other ethnic groups also feel left out of government because President Biya has brought many people from his own Beti ethnic group into government jobs. The UCP uprising, lasting from 1955 to the mid-1960s, drew its support mainly along ethnic lines from the Basa and Bamiléké. Many political parties founded in the 1990s are still informally based on ethnic or regional lines. It can be hoped that some way will be found for ethnicity not to pull Cameroonians apart.

Many Languages

Cameroon has many layers of languages. Each of Cameroon's more than two hundred ethnic groups has its own language

The Baka Pygmies: A Disappearing Ethnic Group

Actually, Pygmy is not the name of an ethnic group. It is a word used to describe people from several ethnic groups in the equatorial African rain forest. The Baka are the main Pygmy group in Cameroon. They are called Pygmies because of their physical appearance. They usually do not grow to more than 4 feet 8 inches (1.45 m), and they have reddish brown skin and tightly curled black hair.

Pygmies are Cameroon's most ancient people. Traditionally, they moved about in small groups, hunting and gathering food in the southern rain forest. Now, loggers and farmers have forced many Pygmies from the rain forest. In addition, the government encourages them to live in settled villages. Some Pygmies have started to marry into Bantu groups. These and other factors have caused a decrease in the Baka Pygmy population. Today, there are only about forty thousand of them left. Government and private programs are attempting to improve Pygmy life in present-day Cameroon. Pygmies are learning how to clear land and to plant and harvest crops. Their children now attend village schools. Pygmy families are also learning how to take better care of their health.

and dialect, which is spoken in homes and villages. Most of these languages do not have a written form. The ethnic languages that have the largest number of speakers are Bamiléké, Ewondo, and Fufulde. Ewondo is spoken by many people in central and southeastern Cameroon. Fufulde is the language of the Fulani.

Cameroon's languages vary from one ethnic group to another.

Common Words and Phrases

English	Bamiléké	Ewondo	Fufulde
Good morning.	ZELL-ay.	BEM-bay kea-ERE.	Pallone e jam.
Good evening.	Oh-BOY.	BEM-bay an-goh-GEE.	Mbaaleene jam.
Good-bye.	Oom-boh.	Oh-kell-em-VUOY.	Pallone e jam.
How are you?	YAH-may-lie?	Oun-VUOY?	No mbaddaa?
Thank you.	Guh-pay-NO.	Ah-boun-ghan.	A jaaraama.

Because Cameroon has so many ethnic languages, just one of those languages could not be chosen as the country's official language. Instead, English and French became Cameroon's official languages. According to the constitution, Cameroon is a bilingual nation. This occurred when the British and French parts of Cameroon united into one country. Cameroonians who speak English are called anglophones; those who speak French are called francophones. Because French Cameroun

This business's sign advertises in both English and French.

was so much larger than the British section, francophones greatly outnumber anglophones.

The government's goal is for all Cameroonians to use both languages. To achieve this goal, students in Cameroon's schools learn both English and French. Besides the educational setting, both languages are used in government and business. In spite of this, Cameroonians resist becoming bilingual. Those who do become bilingual are for the most part graduates of secondary schools and colleges.

So how do Cameroonians communicate with one another? They use what are called *lingua francas*. These are languages that are spoken in the streets and marketplace to conduct everyday business, such as chatting with neighbors or shopping. The three lingua francas are pidgin English, French, and Fufulde. One of the first lingua francas in Cameroon was pidgin English. In the 1800s, Cameroonians used a mixture of English words and words from their own languages to communicate with English traders and missionaries. Pidgin English is still spoken throughout the anglophone area of Cameroon, as well as in southeastern Nigeria. French is the lingua franca for the southern and central part of Cameroon—most of the francophone area. The third lingua franca, Fufulde, is used by the Fulani and people who come in contact with them in northern Cameroon. Over the years, a new form of oral language, called franglais, developed. This language is also called Camfranglais because it combines French and English words with words from ethnic languages. It is spoken mainly in urban areas where francophones and anglophones have contact.

Ibrahim Njoya: Sultan and Scholar

Ibrahim Njoya (1876–1933) was the sixteenth sultan of the Bamoun dynasty. In the early 1900s, he developed alphabet and number systems and a writing form called *shu mom*. Njoya established schools in which shu mom was taught. Njoya used shu mom to write *The History of the Customs and Laws of the Bamouns*. He collected Bamoun tales and legends in written form. He also made a map of Bamoun lands. Originally, shu mom had more than 500 characters. Since then, shu mom has been simplified to eighty-three letters and ten numerals. Shu mom is one of only a few alphabets and scripts developed by Africans for West African languages.

Health and Education

Cameroon's government has made progress in health care and education throughout the country. Between 1983 and 2002, life expectancy in Cameroon rose from forty-four years to fifty-four years. Life expectancy in the United States is about seventy-seven years. The deaths of children less than two

Throughout Cameroon, health clinic care for infants has increased their survival rate.

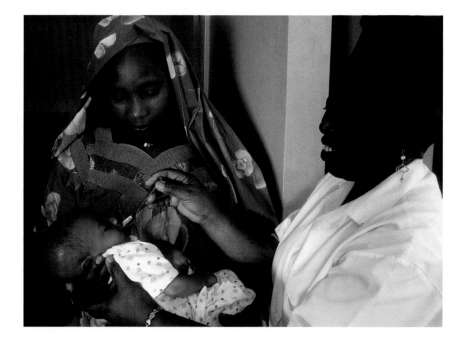

years old decreased from seventy-seven per thousand in 1998 to sixty-nine per thousand in 2002. The infant death rate in the United States is about seven per thousand. Reducing deaths in Cameroon from such common diseases as malaria and sleeping sickness resulted in these improvements.

Cameroon's health care is also changing from a system that emphasized curing diseases to one that tries harder to prevent diseases. Curing diseases means having hospitals, doctors, and nurses to run them, equipment, and drugs, all of which are expensive and extremely limited in Cameroon. Instead, they have started immunizing children with shots against measles and tuberculosis, for example. This reduces diseases, deaths, and medical costs in the future. Programs to provide clean, safe drinking water have also improved the health of many villagers in Cameroon.

Cameroon's health care industry is making strides in caring for people and creating cures for disease and illness.

Classroom enrollment is high in Cameroon. All children ages six through twelve must attend school.

Since independence, Cameroon has reached one of the highest rates of school attendance in Africa. This has occurred because primary education is compulsory from ages six through twelve. Public primary schools are free, and the government assists privately run and religious schools with funds. More than 90 percent of primary-age children attend school. Although about 99 percent of boys are enrolled, only about 82 percent of girls receive even a primary level of education. These percentages drop steeply for secondary enrollments. Only 20 percent of secondary-age students attend school: 23 percent of boys and 18 percent of girls. Most families cannot afford the cost of secondary school tuition, books, and uniforms, which the government doesn't pay for. Many families also do not see the need for further education.

With so few Cameroonians attending secondary school, the number that finish college is even smaller. About 3 percent of Cameroonian men attend college; only 1 percent of women do. The country's major university is the University of Yaoundé. Specialized colleges of law, medicine, and technology are parts of the university. Universities in other cities each specialize in a field of study. For example, the University of Douala offers business courses, the University of Buea trains translators, the University of Dschang has agricultural courses, and the University of Ngaoundéré offers technology programs.

At this point in its history, Cameroon's educated citizens form an elite that find jobs in the government and in the country's businesses. The gap between them and the rest of Cameroonians is quite wide. Although estimates of literacy figures for Cameroon range from 63 to 75 percent, these percentages are for people with only a primary education. Only about 40 percent have literacy levels that are high enough for filling out a job application or reading a newspaper.

Yaoundé University

Traditional Religions, Islam, and Christianity

R ELIGIOUS BELIEFS AND RITUALS PLAY AN IMPORTANT part in the lives of most Cameroonians. Long before Arab Muslims arrived in the north and Christian missionaries came ashore in the south, Cameroon's ethnic groups had developed their own religious practices. Today, close to 40 percent of Cameroonians still practice their traditional religions. Approximately another 40 percent of Cameroonians belong to a Christian church. About another 20 percent follow the beliefs of Islam. Many people who belong to Christian churches or believe in Islam also continue to practice traditional religions.

The Cameroon constitution protects the rights of freedom of religion and worship. Nevertheless, as recently as the

Opposite: **Religious practices have survived in Cameroon for centuries. These women participate in a ritual that represents a journey to the land of the dead.**

These Fulani men are observing an Islamic ritual.

Followers of Religious Beliefs in Cameroon (2000 est.)

Traditional beliefs	40%
Roman Catholics	26.4%
Muslims	21.2%
Protestants	20.7%
Other religious beliefs or no beliefs	8.0%

Note: The total is more than 100 percent because many Cameroonian Christians and Muslims also practice traditional beliefs.

1990s, incidents of police entering churches and arresting and beating worshippers have occurred. The government did not respond to these attacks.

Traditional Religions

Cameroon's traditional religions do not have churches or written scriptures. Instead, Cameroonians who practice these religions believe in three main ideas: a supreme creator god with lesser spirits and deities, the spiritual forces of nature, and the power of ancestors. Each ethnic group has a different name for its creator god. The Bamiléké call him Nso. For the Fang, he is Mebere. Faw is the god of the Fali in northern Cameroon. The creator god is thought to be too important to be concerned with earthly humans, so people do not pray directly to this god. Instead, they pray to lesser spirits or to their ancestors.

It is also believed that the power of ancestors lives in their remains, especially their skulls. The Bamiléké and Fang keep ancestors' remains in special stone jars or wooden containers. At these small shrines, family members offer food, palm oil, or palm wine to their ancestors and pray for good health and rich harvests. Ancestors thus are a link between life and death and between people and natural forces. They are believed to be protectors of their families. Sometimes ancestors show their displeasure with the behavior of their families. This displeasure might be made known in the form of a storm or a poor harvest of crops or other disasters.

Another feature of traditional religions is the belief that natural objects have spiritual forces. For example, a village might have a tree or grove of trees, a mountain, a special rock, or a river that is considered sacred. The villagers may believe that any one of these natural objects is the home of a deity. Sometimes the natural object is thought to be the deity itself.

Some traditional religious groups believe that gods live in rocks and trees.

This diviner is believed to have special powers that can explain the workings of the spirits.

Each ethnic group has some people who are called healers or diviners. They have special skills that help them to explain how or why spiritual forces are at work. When a village or family is having troubles, the diviner might use animal parts to determine the cause of the problem. The diviner may then suggest a way for the family or village to gain favor with an ancestor or deity and thus end the problem. The diviners also determine when special celebrations and ceremonies should take place. Although practicing witchcraft is illegal in Cameroon, traditional religions still believe that some people have the power to do harm and cause evil. Those people are known as witches and sorcerers and are the opposite of healers and diviners. Healers, diviners, witches, and sorcerers practice both in cities and rural villagers.

Islam in Cameroon

The prophet Muhammad founded Islam in A.D. 610 in what is now Saudi Arabia. People who believe in the teachings of Islam are called Muslims. In the A.D. 800s, Arab traders brought Islam for the first time into what is now northern Cameroon. They also carried their religion to other parts of West Africa. Later, in the 1700s, the Fulani Muslims, a West African people, migrated into northern Cameroon. Islam became further established in Cameroon at that time. The major Muslim area in Cameroon is in the north. The area around Foumban in western Cameroon also has a large Muslim population. Many Muslims live in almost all of Cameroon's large cities. Besides the Fulani and Arab groups in Cameroon, the Bamoun and Kanuri ethnic groups also have become followers of Islam.

Muslims pray during the Eid al-Fitr, the end of the holy month of Ramadan.

Like Muslims all over the world, Cameroon's Muslims observe the Five Pillars of Islam. First, they believe in one God, called Allah, with Muhammad as his prophet. Second, they pray five times a day—at sunrise, midmorning, midafternoon, sunset, and night. They are called to prayer by the sound of a horn. Third, they give to the poor. Fourth, they observe daytime fasting during the month of Ramadan. Fifth,

Islamic leaders in Cameroon are lamidos.

if possible, they make a once-in-a-lifetime pilgrimage, called a *hadj*, to Mecca in Saudi Arabia. Mecca is the city of Muhammad's birth. Because making the hadj is very expensive, not all Muslims accomplish it. Those who make it are given a special title. Men are called Hadj; women, Hadjia.

Friday is the Islamic Sabbath. From 11:30 A.M. to 2:30 on Friday afternoons, Muslims gather at their mosques to pray. Men and women do not pray together. Some mosques even have a separate entrance for women. In Cameroon, Islam's leaders are called *lamidos*. Wearing

thick, white turbans and long, flowing, colorful robes called boubous, they lead the people in prayers at the mosques. Villages, towns, and cities with Muslim populations have mosques. Most of Cameroon's major cities have a large mosque, called the Grande Mosquée. Mosques in Cameroon are tall white buildings with narrow towers called *minarets*.

A mosque in northern Cameroon

It is from the minarets that Muslims are called to prayer. All mosques are built so that worshippers face the Muslim holy city of Mecca.

Muslims in Cameroon and throughout the world celebrate three main holy days. The Festival of the Lamb, or Tabaski, remembers how Abraham followed God's command to sacrifice his son Isaac. At the last minute, God told Abraham to spare his son and kill a lamb instead. For Tabaski, every Muslim family is expected to buy a lamb. They are to give one-third of the lamb to the poor, give another third to friends, and roast the last third for their family. The Festival of the Lamb is held at the same time of year as the end of the pilgrimage to Mecca. Muslims thank Allah for the pilgrims' safe return. On Eid al-Moulid, or Muhammad's birthday, Muslims in Cameroon enjoy a day of feasting. Eid al-Fitr is at the end of Ramadan, the month of daytime fasting. On the evening of Eid al-Fitr, Cameroon's Muslims eat rich foods that they have denied themselves for a month.

Important Religious Holidays

Christian Holy Days

Good Friday	Friday before Easter
Easter Sunday	March or April
Ascension Thursday	Forty days from Easter Sunday
Christmas	December 25

Muslim holy days are determined by the Islamic calendar, which is based on a ten-month lunar year. Thus, dates for the holy days vary from year to year.
Festival of the Lamb
Muhammad's Birthday
End of Ramadan

Christian Religions

Cameroonians who practice Christian religions live mainly in cities and villages in the south. The work of Catholic and Lutheran missionaries though, has caused some non-Fulani groups in the north to convert to Christianity. Besides the Lutherans, other major Protestant denominations in Cameroon are Baptists and Presbyterians. About three thousand people work as ministers and teachers and in other roles in the Protestant churches and their missions. In four Protestant theological schools, Cameroonians and other Africans are trained to become ministers. Foreign Protestant missionaries in Cameroon come mainly from the United States, Norway, Canada, and England.

The Roman Catholic Church has five archdioceses and eighteen dioceses in Cameroon. Archbishops preside over the archdioceses of Bamenda, Bertoua, Douala, Garoua, and Yaoundé. Four seminaries train Cameroonians for the priesthood. Several Roman Catholic institutions are in or near Yaoundé. A Benedictine monastery stands atop nearby Mount Fébé. In the center of Yaoundé, people attend Masses in Notre Dame Cathedral, the city's main Roman Catholic church. Separate Masses are said in French, in English, and in some ethnic languages. On the west side of town, an open-air Mass is offered in the Ewondo language each Sunday morning. Traditional Cameroonian music with dancing, drums, and a women's choir are part of this Mass, a colorful mix of Western and African cultures.

Pope John Paul II ordains
new priests during his visit
to Cameroon in 1985.

A most important event for Cameroon's Catholics took place in August 1985, when Pope John Paul II made a four-day papal visit to the country. When he was in Yaoundé, he said Mass in French. When he visited the anglophone city of Bamenda, he said Mass in English.

Besides taking care of Cameroonians' spiritual needs, the Christian churches also minister to their social needs. Many of the country's schools and hospitals are operated by religious groups. Two of Cameroon's better hospitals are Kumbo-Banso Baptist Hospital and Shisong Catholic Hospital. Missions are found in villages throughout Cameroon and near cities in the north. For example, Catholic missions close to Maroua and Garoua provide lodging for travelers. Protestant missions, such as one in Bamenda, also provide lodging.

The main Christian holy days are centered on the life and death of Jesus Christ. Christmas celebrates his birth. Good Friday recalls his death on the cross. Easter rejoices his resurrection from the dead. Ascension Thursday proclaims his ascension in both body and soul to heaven.

Firsts for Two Archbishops of Cameroon

Christian Wiyghan Tumi (1930–present) is Cameroon's first and only cardinal (left). Pope John Paul II appointed him to the College of Cardinals in 1988, while Tumi was archbishop of Garoua. Three years later he became archbishop of Douala. Cardinals hold important positions in the Roman Catholic Church because the College of Cardinals is responsible for electing the popes. Tumi grew up in Kikaikelaki in Southwest Province and received his training for the priesthood in Nigeria, France, and Switzerland.

Paul Verdzekov (1931–present) also accomplished several firsts. In 1970, Pope Paul VI appointed him bishop of Bamenda. When Bamenda became an archdiocese in 1982, Verdzekov was appointed archbishop. Verdzekov was Cameroon's first anglophone bishop and archbishop. He was born in Shisong in Northwest Province and received his training at St. Joseph's College in Buea. Later, he received advanced degrees from the Pontifical University in Rome.

Keeping Rich
Traditions
Alive

THE PEOPLE OF CAMEROON HAVE A LONG AND RICH CULtural heritage. It ranges from traditional carved masks, storytelling, and wooden musical instruments to modern-day abstract art, novels, and popular music on CDs. Cameroonians, like most other African peoples, think of art as part of everyday life. They also believe that people in all levels of society should have access to art. In other words, art should not just be hidden away in museums. Music is meant for community participation, not only for performances in auditoriums or concert halls. Today, Cameroon's writers and artists continue to use many traditional themes and ideas in their works.

Opposite: **Lamido musicians play traditional instruments.**

An elephant dancer wears a heavily beaded mask.

Art: Masks, Sculpture, and Painting

Cameroon's best-known artworks are masks. Each mask is carved from one piece of wood. Some have human faces that resemble a fon, or chief. Others have the faces of such powerful animals, such as elephants, leopards, or buffalo. The masks can be left as plain wood, painted, or completely covered with beads. White paint symbolizes a powerful spirit. Raffia fringe

From Death to Ancestorhood

Among the Bamiléké, female relatives of a dead person announce the death with great wailing. Burial takes place within twenty-four hours and is followed by a week of public mourning. During this time, relatives shave their heads and wear blue or black clothing. A year later, the death ceremonies take place. The deceased person's possessions are put on public display to show what wealth has been passed on to the heirs. At this time, the dead person is considered to have crossed over into the status of ancestorhood. The heirs exhume the body and remove the skull, which is placed in a special wooden box or stone jar to become a family shrine.

sometimes is attached to the masks. Chiefs decide when a mask is to be made and used. Because of this link to the chief, the masks themselves are considered to be powerful. Only men wear the masks. When they put one on, they become the spirit of the mask. They are no longer merely a human but have "become" the mask. No one in the village knows who is wearing the masks because the men are completely covered. Masks are worn either over the face or on top of the head. When masks are worn atop the head, the wearer's face is covered with cloth. The entire body of the mask wearer is also covered in special cloth, with raffia fringe encircling the ankles. Masks are used only at such special ceremonies as to mark a death or to celebrate a harvest. Masks are accompanied at these times by music and dancing. Although many different Cameroonian ethnic groups have made masks, the Bamiléké masks are the most famous.

Other traditional wooden art includes sculptures, stools, house posts, and some musical instruments. Sculptures or statues may represent ancestors or show the close relationship between a mother and child. Special wooden stools are carved for chiefs or other important people. These stools are considered to be seats of power—somewhat like a king's throne. Carved doorframes and house posts, especially among the Bamiléké, mark the homes of important people.

Bronze sculpture is made by using the lost wax method. A sculpture made of wax is encased or molded in clay. When the clay dries, the mold is heated, causing the wax to melt and run out. The wax is replaced with hot, liquid bronze. When the bronze has cooled and the clay mold is broken, a beautiful sculpture is revealed.

Today, many of Cameroon's artists continue to use many traditional techniques and themes. Modern-day wood-carvers often use themes reflecting Cameroon's history. The pieces show scenes from hunts, wars, and religious ceremonies. Other artists' works illustrate the unity of all the Cameroonian people. Giddeon Mpando's *Reunification Monument* in Yaoundé includes children from Cameroon's different ethnic groups. Another of his works stands in Yaoundé's city hall. It depicts the unity of the Cameroonian family. Hervé Youmbi is best known for his bold, colorful portraits of such African leaders as Nelson Mandela and Kofi Annan. Youmbi is also recognized for his works using mask images.

Storytelling and Written Books

Storytelling takes place throughout Cameroon—in cities as well as villages. Unlike as in many other African countries,

This throne was made for Cameroonian chief Mene around 1930.

storytellers in Cameroon are not professional performers. Instead, anyone who can recite, sing, or act out a tale and can interact with an audience can be a storyteller. Housewives, children, farmers, laborers, traders, nurses, and teachers are a few kinds of people who are storytellers in Cameroon. Through storytelling, Cameroonians are able to keep a connection with their history and the community. The tales, legends, and myths pass down values and knowledge of their group's history and culture. Sometimes a tale is told to

Storytellers are common in Cameroon. Here, a father tells his son a story.

resolve a family or community problem, in the way that fables can make a point.

Cameroonian storytellers mainly tell three kinds of tales. First, there are tales that usually concern the ordinary roles of men and women, such as "The Boy Who Falsely Swore on the Shrine" or "The Wicked Co-wife." Another kind of tale explains how things came to be, such as "Why Tortoise Has Cracks on His Shell" or "How Lake Mo Came into Being." Trickster tales are a third kind of story. The trickster can be a human or animal character that uses quick wit to sidestep danger. Storytelling usually takes place in the evening when the day's work is done. In rural areas, storytelling is an especially popular form of entertainment during the dry season after the harvest is done.

Today, many Cameroonians tell stories through novels. Most of them are written in French or English. Anticolonial themes are common in Cameroonian novels, such as Kenjo Jumban's *White Man of God* and Ferdinand Oyono's *Houseboy*. Other themes include finding one's personal identity and dealing with the changing roles of men and women in society. Francis Bebey (1929–2001) was one of Cameroon's most popular writers. Characters in his books are able to bring together elements of traditional and modern cultures. In this way, writers form identities within the modern world without giving up their cherished connection to the past. Bebey's best-known novel is *Agatha Moudio's Son*. Calixthe Beyala has written several novels that deal with women's struggles within the traditional family and in society. Her best-known books are *It Is the Sun That Has Burnt Me* and *Only the Devil Knew*.

Mongo Beti: One of Africa's Most Powerful Writers

Mongo Beti was born Alexandre Biyidi-Awala in 1932, near Yaoundé. He was brought up Roman Catholic and attended a Catholic mission school. From there, he went to high school in Yaoundé and later graduated from the Sorbonne University in Paris with a doctorate in modern language. In 1954, he used the pen name Eza Boto when he published his first novel, *Cruel City*. In 1956, he adopted the pen name Mongo Beti. Under this name, he published *Poor Christ of Bomba*, *Mission to Kala*, and *King Lazarus*. These books criticized colonial missionaries in all African countries. After Cameroon gained independence, Mongo Beti's books attacked the new government. Because of this criticism Mongo Beti's books were banned in Cameroon, and he spent many years in exile in France. Mongo Beti returned to Cameroon in 1992. Before he died in 2001, *Too Much Sun Kills Love* was published. This book attacks dictatorships, but in a comical way.

Music

Musical instruments in Cameroon can be traced back hundreds of years. The balafon is a wooden xylophone with fifteen to nineteen wooden keys, each suspended over a hollow gourd. A player, who is usually seated, strikes the keys with a wooden hammer. Different kinds of balafons make different sounds. One called the talker sounds like a human voice. The bass balafon produces a deep, drumlike sound. The *mvet*, or harp-zither, is a stringed instrument that is plucked. This

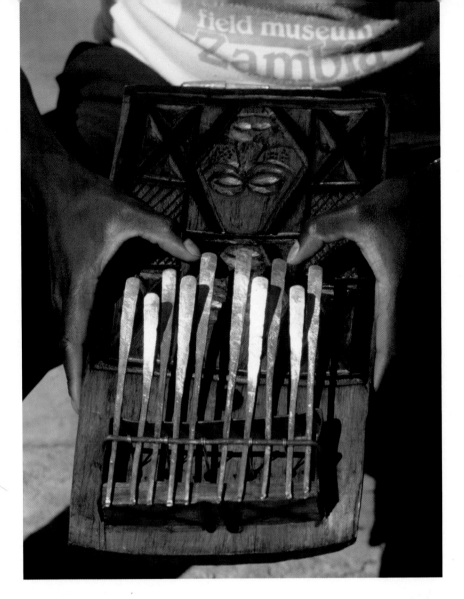

Thumb piano

instrument sometimes is played during the telling of a story. Thumb pianos are sets of metal or wooden keys of various lengths that are attached to a board. The player uses his thumbs to twang the keys. These traditional instruments are used in modern bands in Cameroon. The writer Francis Bebey, who was also a musician, was accomplished on the thumb piano. Many kinds of drums are also played in Cameroon.

The balafon, zither, thumb piano, and drums are mainly played by men. Wooden flutes are reserved for women to play. An unusual sound is achieved by putting water in the flute before it is played. Women standing in lakes or rivers can make drumlike sounds. They strike the surface of the water in a specific way with their hands.

Cameroon is especially known for two kinds of modern music: makossa and bikutsi. Makossa started in the Douala area and means "make me dance" in the Duala language. It has a smooth sound that blends soul, swing, jazz, and Congo beats. Francis Bebey was a popular makossa star, too. But it was Manu Dibango (1933–) who made Cameroon's makossa world famous. His album *Soul Makossa* sold more than 1 million copies in 1972, and he enjoys popular success to this day. Bikutsi music can be traced back to the balafon music of the Beti people. It developed into a popular music in Yaoundé. Bikutsi, which means "hit or pound the ground," has a definite pounding beat.

Sports

Sports is such an important part of Cameroonian life that the government has a ministry of youth and sports. This ministry regulates sports at all levels of education. Sports such as boxing, soccer, and volleyball have their own regulating groups. These groups work with the sports ministry. Cameroonians enjoy many other sports, including canoeing, hiking, running, swimming, and wrestling.

Cameroon also holds international sporting events. Each year at the end of January or early in February, Buea is headquarters for the Race of Hope. About five hundred runners race about 25 miles (40 km) from Buea to the top of Mount Cameroon and back to town. The runners come from all over the world, including the United States, Europe, and other African countries. Winning men finish the race in about four and one-half hours; women complete it in about five and one-half hours. At the same time, Cameroon hosts a cycling race. Bicyclists peddle hard between Douala and Limbe and back.

Sports are encouraged in Cameroon. Here, neighborhood boys play an informal game of soccer.

Cameroon's national soccer team played in the FIFA Confederation Cup in France in 2003.

Soccer, though, is the national sport. Informal games take place in city neighborhoods and in villages everywhere. Cameroon's cities also support professional teams that play one another. The Indomitable Lions is the national soccer team. In recent years, the team has filled Cameroonians with patriotic pride. In 2000, the Indomitable Lions won the gold medal for soccer at the Olympic Games in Sydney, Australia.

When they beat Spain in a close game, the team brought home Cameroon's first Olympic medal—the gold! The Lions have played in World Cup games since 1982. They have also performed well elsewhere in Africa. The team has won the African Nations Cup for Cameroon four times—1984, 1988, 2000, and 2002.

Africa's Soccer Player of the Century

Being named player of the year in a sport is a great honor. Imagine how Roger Milla felt in May 2000 when he was named Africa's soccer player of the century—for the twentieth century. Milla was born in 1952 in Cameroon. He is best known for his performances in World Cup games. He led the Indomitable Lions to Cameroon's first World Cup games in 1982. In 1990, he led them to the quarter finals of the World Cup. That was the first time an African team had made it that far. In the 1994 World Cup, the team didn't get beyond the first round. Milla, however, scored a goal, becoming the oldest player to score at a World Cup. Today, Milla is retired and divides his time between Cameroon and France, where he has a soccer training camp for young people.

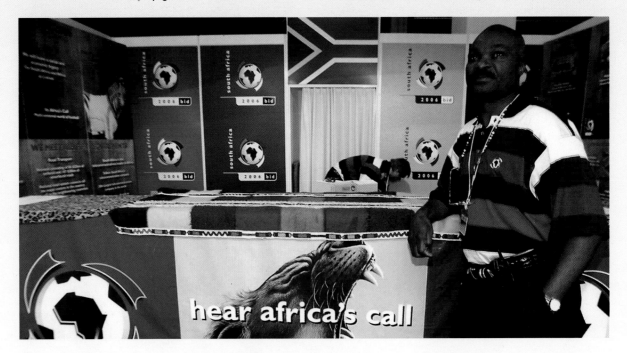

Everyday Life

C AMEROON'S WIDE VARIETY OF ETHNIC GROUPS, LAN-
guages, religions, climates, and vegetation zones has resulted
in many ways of life. Cameroonians eat a great number of different foods, live in many types of homes, and wear
distinctive, colorful clothing. Although they celebrate numerous traditional festivals, their national independence has
added important new holidays.

Opposite: **An outdoor market provides goods needed for daily meals.**

Eating in Cameroon

In traditional homes, men eat first, then the women, and finally
the children. In each of these groups, the oldest are served first.
Hand washing is an important ritual before the meal. Food is
eaten with the fingers, and Cameroonians use only their right
hand for eating. Most food is dipped from a common bowl, a
practice found in many cultures around the world.

The traditional eating style in Cameroon includes eating with the right hand.

This woman cooks fish in the market.

Most Cameroonians who can afford it have three meals a day. Breakfast for villagers might consist of dried or smoked fish and tea, chocolate, or coffee. In the city, Cameroonians might eat scrambled eggs, fried potatoes, and bread. Their favorite beverage is café au lait, coffee with hot milk. About noon, villagers usually eat a lunch of rice in a spicy sauce. Lunchtime in the cities is closer to 1:00 P.M. Cameroonians in cities might have *fufu*, soup, stew, or plantains for lunch. Plantains are similar to bananas but are boiled, fried, or roasted before eating. Dinner is in the evening between 7:00 P.M. and 8:30 P.M. People in villages usually have yams or plantains added to whatever was leftover from lunch. Chicken or beef and rice might be served for dinner in cities. Throughout Cameroon such fruits as bananas,

Special Foods in Cameroon

Achu (right) is a dish made in the northwest. Mashed cocoyams (taro) are formed into a mound like a volcano with a crater in the middle. A sauce of palm oil and hot pepper is placed in the crater. Diners use one finger to scoop up the cocoyam and dip it in the sauce before popping it into their mouth.

Fufu is made of pounded corn, plantain, cassava, or cocoyams. It has the consistency of a dumpling and is served in a common dish. Cameroonians make a small ball of it with their right hand and press their thumb in to make a depression. Then they scoop soup, stew, fish, or vegetables into the depression, place the fufu in their mouth, and swallow it whole. Fufu is not supposed to be chewed.

Jammu-jammu is a thick vegetable stew that is eaten with fufu.

mangoes, papayas, and oranges are eaten as snacks or passed around after a meal.

Although large amounts of tea, coffee, and cocoa are grown in Cameroon, most Cameroonians prefer milk, fruit drinks, and soda. Such instant drinks as Nescafé and Ovaltine are popular, though. Beer and palm wine are also well liked among adults. Palm wine, which comes from palm trees, is very sweet and quite strong.

Recipe for Egussi Stew

In this recipe, pumpkin seeds are used instead of egussi seeds, as they taste much alike.

Ingredients

2 large peeled and chopped tomatoes

$\frac{1}{2}$ cup chopped flat parsley

1 teaspoon ginger powder

3 thinly sliced garlic cloves

1 hot pepper, seeded and chopped

2 chopped onions

1 tablespoon celery seed

$2\frac{1}{2}$ cups water

3 tablespoons vegetable oil

$1\frac{1}{2}$ pounds stewing beef, cut into bite-size pieces

1 tablespoon salt

1 cup shelled pumpkin seeds

Preparation

1. Place tomatoes, parsley, ginger, garlic, hot pepper, half of chopped onions, celery seed, and $\frac{1}{4}$ cup water in blender or food processor. Blend until mixture becomes liquid.

2. In a heavy saucepan, heat the vegetable oil over medium-high heat. Add the rest of the chopped onion and cook until light brown. Add the stewing beef and cook until browned, stirring frequently.

3. Pour the mixture from the blender into the saucepan and add salt to taste. Slightly cover the pan and cook over medium heat until most of the liquid is gone.

4. Add two cups of water to the saucepan. Bring to a boil, then lower heat to simmer, or low.

5. In a heavy bowl, pour $\frac{1}{4}$ cup of water over the pumpkin seeds. Mash until a paste forms.

6. Add the pumpkin seed paste to the stew and stir. Continue stirring and cooking about 20 minutes longer. (The stew should be a bit lumpy.) Ladle the stew into soup bowls. Enjoy!

Egussi is sometimes served over rice.

Clothing

Because Cameroon has so many different ethnic groups and climates, there is no one national dress or costume. One kind of ethnic dress that is well known in Cameroon is made of the blue and white cloth of the Bamiléké. Today, this traditional cloth is made in Fulani textile mills. It is worn for special ceremonies.

Both traditional and Western styles of dress are worn throughout the country. People in the cities tend to wear Western-style clothing at school, work, and at home.

Traditional dress in the south consists of a long skirt called a *pagne*. This consists of several yards of cloth that is wrapped around the body. Women might wear a blouse or T-shirt with the pagne. Men wear a looser version of this skirt over long pants. They might wear short-sleeved shirts or T-shirts. In Muslim areas, both men and women wear clothes that cover most of their bodies. Throughout Cameroon, women wear colorful scarves, headdresses, or turbans. Women in the northern village of Tourou are known for their calabash (gourd) hats. Symbols on the hats sometimes show whether a woman is married or single and if she has children.

Hair grooming is important to both men and women in Cameroon. Men use combs with long teeth and a long handle. They were once made of wooden sticks tied together with raffia. Now most are made of plastic. In villages, Cameroonian women take turns styling one another's hair.

This woman dresses in the traditional pagne.

Women usually comb and braid each other's hair in the villages of Cameroon.

They make intricate braids and weave beads into their hair. Some women are professional hair stylists and have booths or shops in the local markets.

Housing

Housing also varies throughout Cameroon. In the grasslands, Bamiléké homes are made of wood from palm trees. Any cracks in the square walls are filled in with mud or dried clay. Over these walls is a tall cone-shaped thatched roof. On the savanna, many round homes are made of baked mud. They also have thatched roofs. In the dry northern land homes are sculpted completely from clay. Homes do not stand alone in

Bamiléké tribal huts are made of wood and dried clay.

Cameroon. Instead, they are part of family compounds. Within ethnic groups that practice polygamy, one man may have several wives. In his compound, each wife has her own house in which to raise her children.

Although many Cameroonians still live in traditional-style housing, many of these homes no longer exist. They have been replaced with buildings made of concrete blocks, or breeze blocks—cement blocks made partly from the ashes and

Concrete and cement homes are replacing traditional housing in Cameroon.

Housing in the Village of Tos

Tos is a remote small village at the foot of a volcanic mountain in western Cameroon. It is a village of thatched-roof houses, both round and square. The women and children live in the round houses; the men, in the square ones. Storytellers in Tos say that many years ago, after the last eruption of the volcano, only two houses—one round and one square—were left standing in the village. The chief told all the women to live in the round house and the men to live in the square one. When they rebuilt the village, the men and women continued to live separately. Today, young people who leave Tos find out how unusual their village is.

Driving in Cameroon

Few people own cars in Cameroon, and railroads mainly connect large cities. For these reasons, most Cameroonians use taxis to get from town to town. The taxis are actually minibuses. Each town has a motor park where the taxis load their passengers. When enough people are onboard, the taxi sets out. Once on the road, the taxi might have to stop for a roadblock. Roadblocks are a common occurrence throughout Cameroon. They are usually set up outside of towns, and their main purpose is to enrich the local police. Even if drivers have done nothing wrong, they usually must pay a bribe to continue on their way. In this way, government corruption reaches the average Cameroonian.

small bits left when making charcoal. They have corrugated tin roofs and iron grillwork trim. Most cities provide modern housing with private homes or small apartment buildings. As in most countries, parts of Cameroon's cities are run down and unsafe. To improve the housing situation, the government plans to build 100,000 homes within the next ten years.

Festivals and Holidays

Ethnic groups and villages throughout Cameroon have special celebrations. Each November, a famous horse-racing festival

Carry It

"Carry it" is a game children play in many of Cameroon's villages. In this game, several players stand in a circle and hold hands. They chose a leader who calls out each player's name in turn. The leader says, "Paul, carry it." Paul then lifts his right leg and puts it over his right hand. He stands on one leg, resting the back of his knee on his and his neighbor's hands. When all the players have been called, everyone is left standing on one foot. The whole group then chants "Carry it! Carry it!" and hops on their left feet. The game ends when they lose their balance and break the circle.

takes place in Kumbo, a grasslands town of the Banso people. Canoe racing takes place in Limbe's coastal waters between December and March. During the racing season, people from nearby villages perform traditional music and dances onshore. Wrestling tournaments are part of the traditional Bakweri culture. They take place in Fako in the dry season in village, division, and subdivision levels.

Two national holidays are celebrated with parades, speeches, and other festivities throughout Cameroon. On February 11, the nation celebrates Youth Day. Cameroonian youth in their school uniforms parade down the nation's cities streets. One year the parade in Yaoundé lasted five hours. At one time, February 11 was National Day. That was the date in 1961 when the people in Southern British Cameroons voted to become part of the Federal Republic of Cameroon. On that day in 1972, Cameroonians voted to become the United Republic of Cameroon. Now, National Day is celebrated on May 20. The parades and speeches are held to promote the feeling of national unity.

National Holidays in Cameroon

New Year's Day	January 1
Youth Day	February 11
Labor Day	May 1
National Day	May 20
Christmas	December 25

Timeline

Cameroon History		World History	
People are living in what is now Cameroon.	About 50,000 B.C.E.		
		2500 B.C.	Egyptians build the Pyramids and the Sphinx in Giza.
		563 B.C.	The Buddha is born in India.
Sao civilization develops in what is now northern Cameroon.	A.D. 400s–1600s	A.D. 313	The Roman emperor Constantine recognizes Christianity.
		610	The Prophet Muhammad begins preaching a new religion called Islam.
		1054	The Eastern (Orthodox) and Western (Roman) Churches break apart.
		1066	William the Conqueror defeats the English in the Battle of Hastings.
		1095	Pope Urban II proclaims the First Crusade.
		1215	King John seals the Magna Carta.
		1300s	The Renaissance begins in Italy.
		1347	The Black Death sweeps through Europe.
		1453	Ottoman Turks capture Constantinople, conquering the Byzantine Empire.
Portuguese explorers name the Wouri River "Rio dos Camarões."	1472	1492	Columbus arrives in North America.
Bamoun dynasty is founded in what is now western Cameroon.	1400s	1500s	The Reformation leads to the birth of Protestantism.
		1776	The Declaration of Independence is signed.
		1789	The French Revolution begins.
Modibo Adama founds the Adamawa Kingdom.	1806		
Cameroonian chiefs frequently ask to become a British Protectorate but are turned down.	1833–1881		
Cameroon becomes the German Protectorate of Kamerun.	1884	1865	The American Civil War ends.
Yaoundé is founded as a German military post.	1890		
Kamerun becomes involved in World War I.	1914–1916	1914	World War I breaks out.

Cameroon History

British and French defeat the Germans and divide Kamerun into British Cameroons and French Cameroun.	1916
The League of Nations grants Britain and France mandates over their parts of Cameroon.	1922
Cameroonians serve in the French army and also help in the British war effort in World War II.	1939–1945
The British and French mandates become trusteeships.	1946
Britain and France begin giving their parts of Cameroon self-government.	1954–1955
Nationalist uprising begins in French Cameroun.	1955
Independent Republic of Cameroun is formed; Ahmadou Ahidjo is elected president.	1960
Federal Republic of Cameroon is formed with reunification of Cameroun Republic and British Southern Cameroons.	1961
United Republic of Cameroon is formed.	1972
President Ahidjo resigns and Paul Biya becomes president of Cameroon.	1982
Paul Biya is elected president of Cameroon.	1984
Multiparty system is approved.	1990
Cameroon's first multiparty presidential and National Assembly elections are held; President Biya is reelected but the CPDM party loses its majority.	1992
Cameroon joins the British Commonwealth of Nations.	1995
The Republic of Cameroon adopts a new constitution.	1996
In national elections, President Paul Biya is reelected and the CPDM party regains its majority in the National Assembly.	1997
Cameroonian and Nigerian leaders hold talks about the Bakassi Peninsula boundary dispute.	2003

World History

1917	The Bolshevik Revolution brings communism to Russia.
1929	Worldwide economic depression begins.
1939	World War II begins, following the German invasion of Poland.
1945	World War II ends.
1957	The Vietnam War starts.
1969	Humans land on the moon.
1975	The Vietnam War ends.
1979	Soviet Union invades Afghanistan.
1983	Drought and famine begin in Africa.
1989	The Berlin Wall is torn down, as communism crumbles in Eastern Europe.
1991	Soviet Union breaks into separate states.
1992	Bill Clinton is elected U.S. president.
2000	George W. Bush is elected U.S. president.
2001	Terrorists attack World Trade Towers, New York, and the Pentagon, Washington, D.C.

Fast Facts

Official name: Republic of Cameroon, République du Cameroun

Capital: Yaoundé

Official languages: English, French

Yaoundé

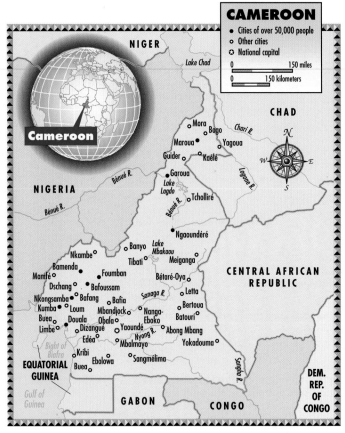

Cameroon's flag

Cameroon Mountains

Official religion:	None
Year of founding:	1960, independence; 1972, unitary republic
National anthem:	"O Cameroun, Berceau de Nos Ancêtres" ("O Cameroon, Thou Cradle of Our Fathers"); music by Samuel Minkyo Bamba and words by Moise Nyatte Nkoro
Government:	Unitary, multiparty republic
Chief of state:	President
Head of government:	Prime minister
Area and dimensions:	183,569 square miles (475,442 sq km)
Latitude and longitude of geographic center:	6° North, 12° East
Land and water borders:	Lake Chad to the north, Chad and Central African Republic to the east, Republic of the Congo to the southeast and south, Gabon and Equatorial Guinea to the south, Nigeria and the Bight of Biafra in the Gulf of Guinea to the west
Highest elevation:	Mount Cameroon at 13,435 feet (4,095 m) above sea level
Lowest elevation:	Sea level at the coastline
Average annual temperatures:	82°F (27.8°C) in January; 70°F (21.1°C) in July
Average annual precipitation:	100 inches (254 cm)
National population (2002 est.):	16,184,748

Waza National Park

Currency

Population of largest cities:

Douala (1995)	1,320,000
Yaoundé (1999)	1,120,000
Garoua (1992)	160,000
Maroua (1992)	140,000
Bafoussam (1992)	120,000

Famous landmarks:

- ▶ *Beaches of Limbe*, on the northwestern coast
- ▶ *Dja Reserve*, in the southeast
- ▶ *Korup National Park*, in the southwest
- ▶ *Manengouba Crater Lakes*, in the southwest
- ▶ *Mount Cameroon*, in the southwest
- ▶ *Museum of Cameroonian Art*, Yaoundé
- ▶ *Royal Palace and Museum*, Foumban
- ▶ *Waza National Park*, in the north

Industry: Oil production and refining are Cameroon's main industries. Other important mineral resources are bauxite for making aluminum products and iron ore. Food processing, lumber processing, and the manufacture of textiles are other leading Cameroonian industries.

Currency: Basic monetary unit, CFAF (CFA franc); U.S. $1 equals CFAF 597 (September 2003)

System of weights and measures: Metric system

Literacy rate: 79 percent (2003 est.)

Cameroonian boys

Common words and phrases:

English	Bamiléké	Ewondo	Fufulde
Good morning	*ZELL-ay.*	*BEM-bay kea-ERE.*	*Pallone e jam.*
Good evening.	*Oh-BOY.*	*BEM-bay an-goh-GEE.*	*Mbaaleene jam.*
Good-bye.	*Oom-boh.*	*Oh-kell-em-VUOY*	*Pallone e jam.*
How are you?	*YAH-may-lie?*	*Oun-VUOY?*	*No mbaddaa?*
Thank you.	*Guh-pay-NO.*	*Ah-boun-ghan.*	*A jaaraama.*

Famous Cameroonians:

Modibo Adama (1786–1847)
Founder of Adamawa Kingdom

Ahmadou Ahidjo (1924–1989)
Cameroon's first president

Francis Bebey (1929–2001)
Writer and musician

Mongo Beti (1932–2001)
(Alexandre Biyidi-Awala)
Writer

Paul Biya (1933–)
Cameroon's second president

Manu Dibango (1933–)
Musician

Roger Milla (1952–)
Africa's soccer player of the century

Delphine Zanga Tsogo Tsang (1935–)
*Cameroon's first female
government minister*

Christian Wiyghan Tumi (1930–)
*Roman Catholic cardinal,
archbishop of Douala*

Reuben Um Nyobe (1913–1958)
*Nationalist leader for
Cameroon independence*

Roger Milla

To Find Out More

Books

▶ Fitzpatrick, Mary. *West Africa*. 5th ed. Victoria, Australia: Lonely Planet Publications, 2002.

▶ Hathaway, Jim. *Cameroon in Pictures*. Visual Geography Series. Minneapolis, Minn: Lerner Publications Company, 1999.

▶ Sheehan, Sean. *Cameroon*. Cultures of the World Series. New York: Marshall Cavendish, 2001.

▶ Tchana, Katrin. *Sense Pass King: A Story from Cameroon*. New York: Holiday House, 2002.

▶ Weaver-Gelzer, Charlotte. *In the Time of Trouble*. New York: Dutton Children's Books, 1993.

Audio Recordings

▶ *Cameroon: Baka Pygmy Music*. UNESCO label, 2000. Audio CD with ten tracks of instrumental music and vocal chanting, including singing by children.

▶ *Cameroon: Bikutsi Tempo*. Sonodisc label, 1997. Audio CD with nine tracks by various popular artists.

▶ *Cameroon: Flutes of the Mandara Mountains*. Ocora label, 1997. Audio CD with nineteen tracks of hunting, harvest, rain, and dance songs.

Web Sites

▶ **Cameroon on the Digital Edge**
www.cmclick.com
Links to information on Cameroon's geography, languages, economy, history, and travel.

▶ **Cameroon Soccer Page**
www.geocities.com/balioldboy
Web site devoted to Cameroon's Indomitable Lions, with a history of the team, players' profiles, and interviews with players.

▶ **Elephants of Cameroon**
www.fieldtripearth.org
A project in Cameroon sponsored by the North Carolina Zoological Park. It includes a calendar of events, description of the project's activities, diary entries of the project's participants, and e-mail links for asking questions.

▶ **Limbe Botanical and Zoological Garden**
www.mcbcclimbe.org/home.shtml
Text and photos of Cameroonian plants and animals.

Organizations and Embassies

▶ **Embassy of the Republic of Cameroon**
2349 Massachusetts Avenue NW
Washington, D.C. 20008
202-265-8790

▶ **U.S. Embassy in Cameroon**
Rue Nachtigal, BP 817
Yaoundé, Cameroon
237-22-2589

Index

Page numbers in *italics* indicate illustrations.

Meet the Author

P ATRICIA K. KUMMER writes and edits textbook materials and nonfiction books for children and young adults at her home office in Lisle, Illinois. She earned a bachelor of arts in history from the College of St. Catherine, St. Paul, Minnesota, and a master of arts degree in history from Marquette University, Milwaukee, Wisconsin. Before starting her career in publishing, she taught social studies at the junior high/middle school level.

She has written books about American, African, Asian, and European history. She wrote *Côte d'Ivoire*, *Ukraine*, *Tibet*, and *Singapore* in the Children's Press series Enchantment of the World. One of her favorite projects was writing a commissioned biography for Jerry Reinsdorf, chairman of the Chicago Bulls and Chicago White Sox. The biography commemorates the life of his administrative assistant who died, leaving a three-year-old daughter. The book was based totally on interviews. It will be presented to the daughter when she is about thirteen years old.

"Writing books about people, states, and countries requires a great deal of research," she says. "To me, researching is the most fun part of a project. My method of research begins by going online. First, I clicked on amazon.com to compile a list of the most recent books on Cameroon. From there, I went to my public library. For the books my library didn't have, I placed interlibrary loan requests. To keep up with events in Cameroon, I checked the Cameroon News Web site for daily news reports. I also found several other informative Web sites."

Ms. Kummer hopes that this book will help young people better understand how the nation of Cameroon came to be and how it is still working on establishing a national identity.

Photo Credits